OCT 1 2 2005

The Couriers
03
The Ballad of Johnny Funwrecker

D1532684

Other titles by Brian Wood and Rob G:

THE COURIERS
THE COURIERS 02: DIRTBIKE MANIFESTO

Also by Brian Wood:

CHANNEL ZERO
PUBLIC DOMAIN: A CHANNEL ZERO DESIGNBOOK

COUSCOUS EXPRESS
(with Brett Weldele)

DEMO
THE DEMO SCRIPTBOOK
CHANNEL ZERO: JENNIE ONE
(with Becky Cloonan)

THE TOURIST
(with Toby Cypress)

Available From AiT/Planet Lar

The Couriers 03: The Ballad of Johnny Funwrecker
By Brian Wood and Rob G

Published by AiT/Planet Lar, 2034 47th Avenue, San Francisco, CA 94116
All Rights Reserved

First Edition January 2005

10 9 8 7 6 5 4 3 2 1

The Couriers 03: The Ballad of Johnny Funwrecker is © 2005 Brian Wood
Cover illustrations by Rob G. Cover and book design by Brian Wood
Lettered by Ryan Yount. Production By Whiskey Island

ISBN: 1-932051-31-7

The Couriers
03
The Ballad of Johnny Funwrecker
BY BRIAN WOOD AND ROB G

AIT★PLANET LAR

SAN FRANCISCO

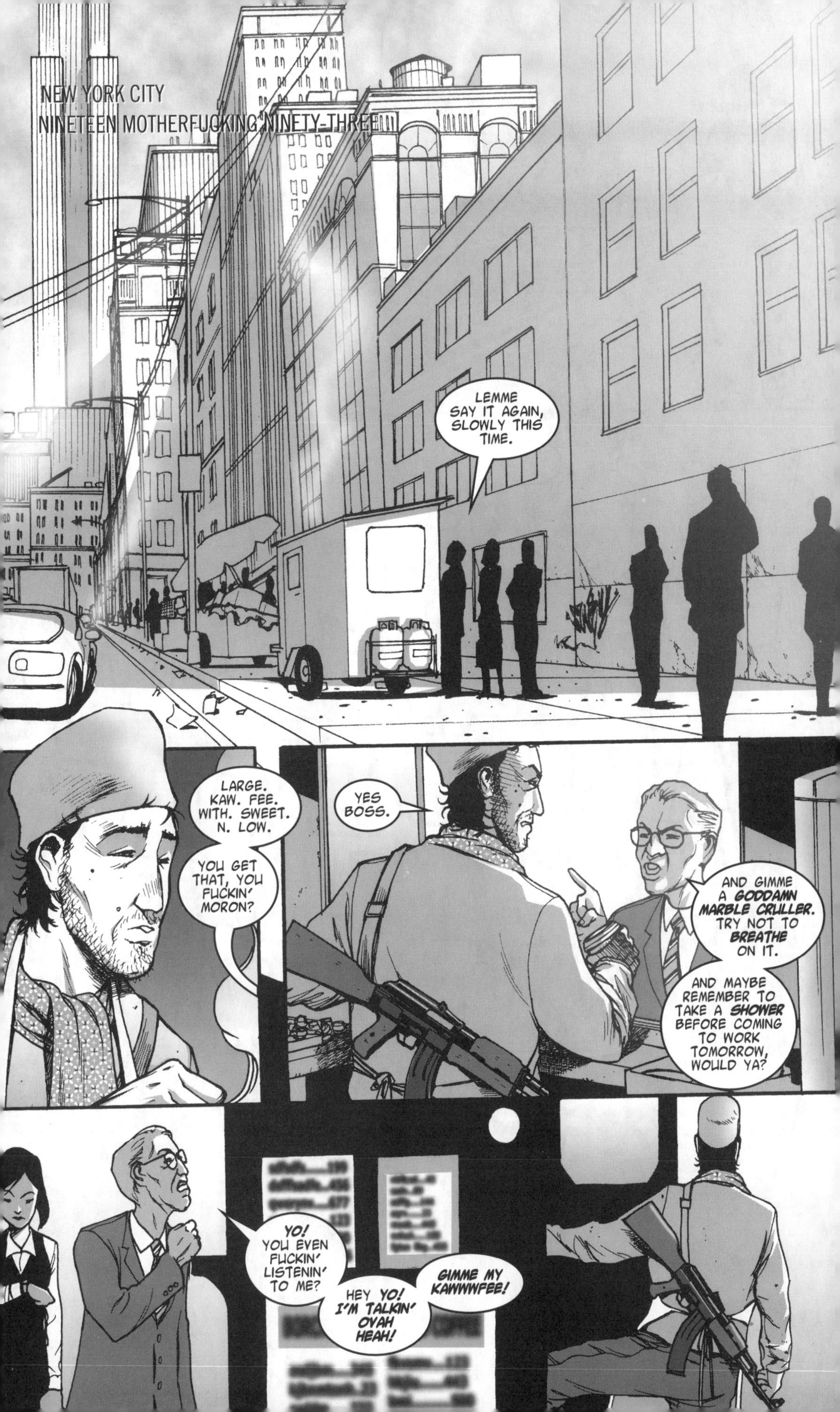
NEW YORK CITY
NINETEEN MOTHERFUCKING NINETY-THREE
LEMME SAY IT AGAIN, SLOWLY THIS TIME.
LARGE. KAW. FEE. WITH. SWEET. N. LOW.
YOU GET THAT, YOU FUCKIN' MORON?
YES BOSS.
AND GIMME A GODDAMN MARBLE CRULLER. TRY NOT TO BREATHE ON IT.
AND MAYBE REMEMBER TO TAKE A SHOWER BEFORE COMING TO WORK TOMORROW, WOULD YA?
YO! YOU EVEN FUCKIN' LISTENIN' TO ME?
HEY YO! I'M TALKIN' OVAH HEAH!
GIMME MY KAWWWFEE!

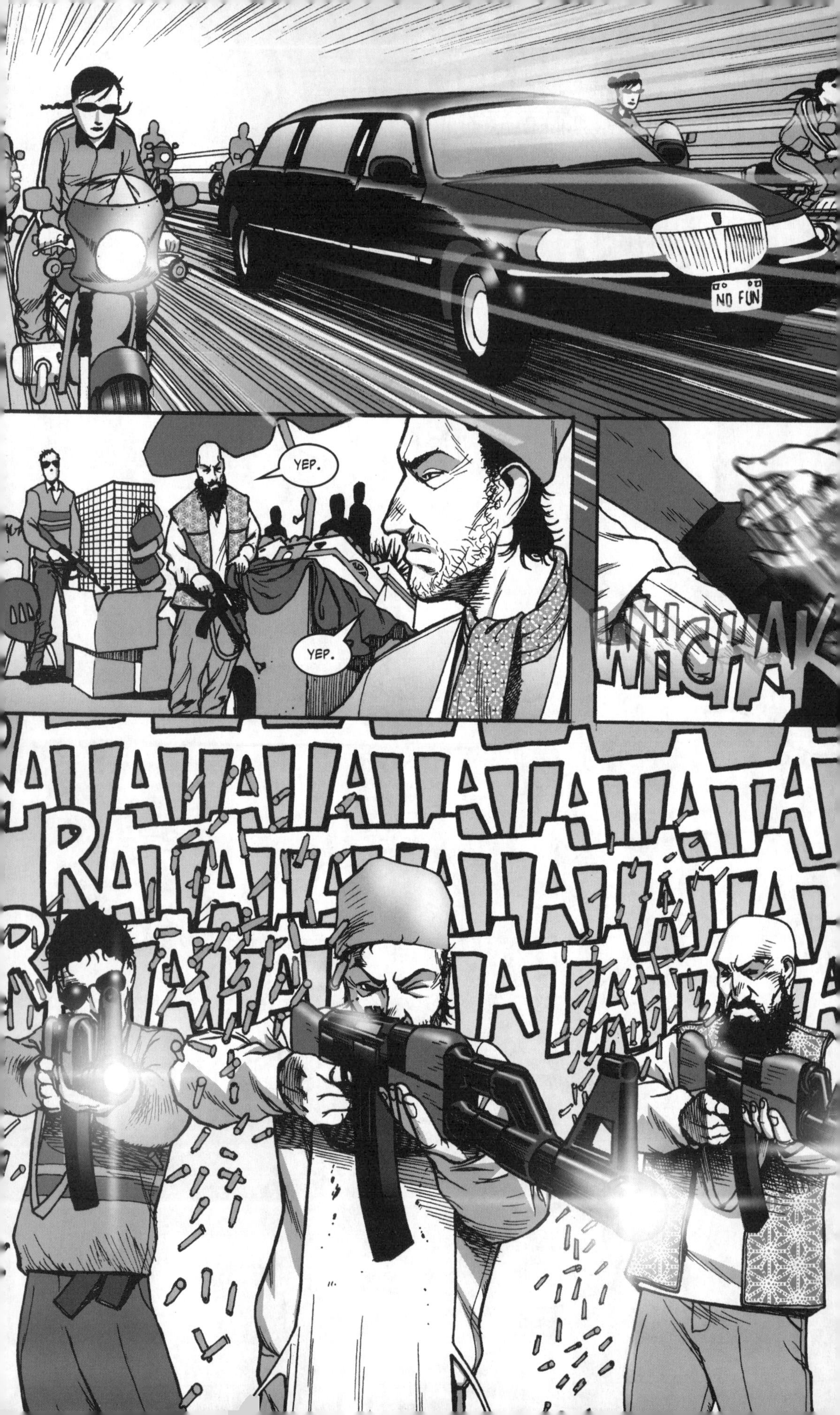
NO FUN
YEP.
YEP.
WHCHAK

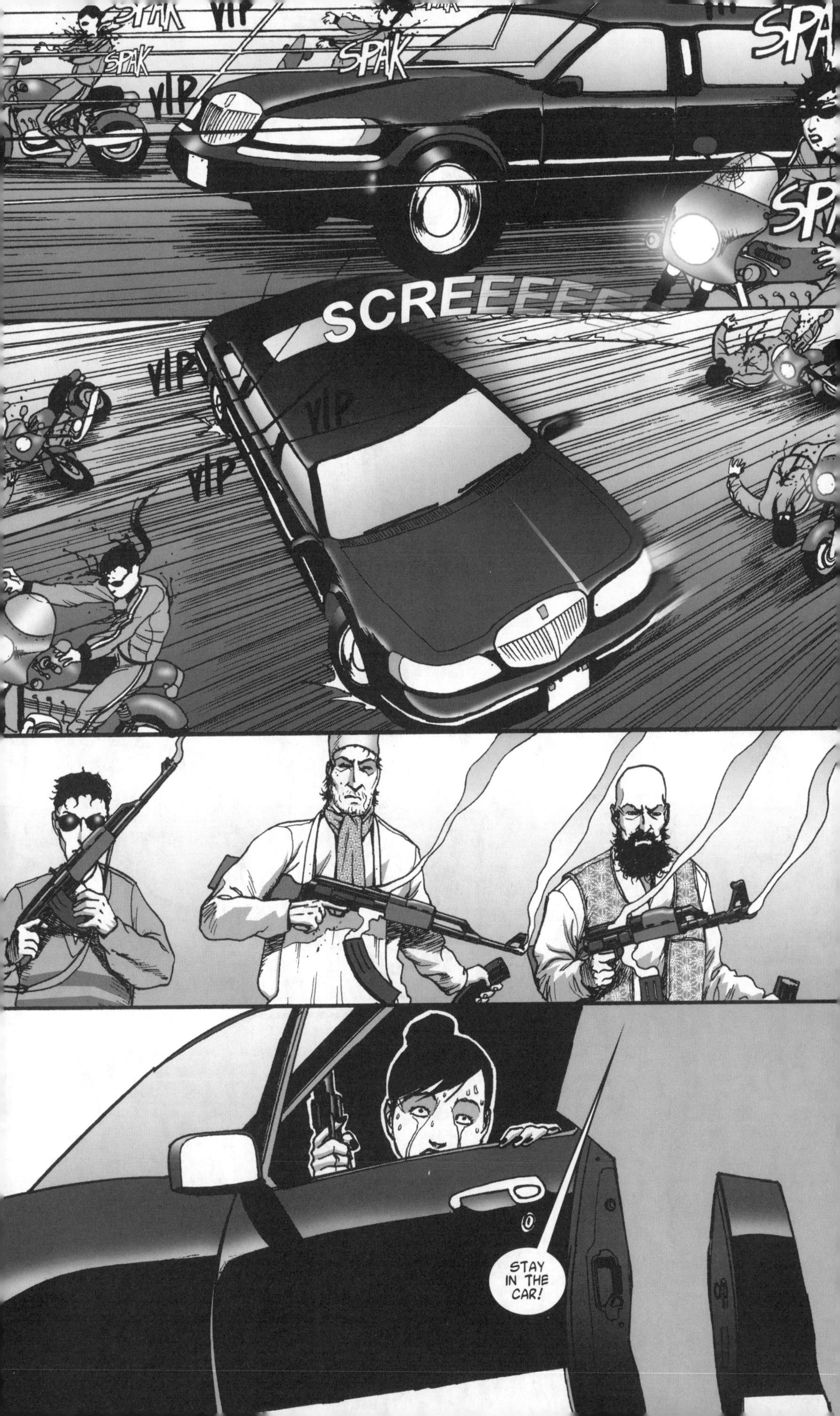

VIP
SPAK
VIP
SPAK
SPAK
SPAK
SCREEEEEE
VIP
VIP
VIP
STAY IN THE CAR!

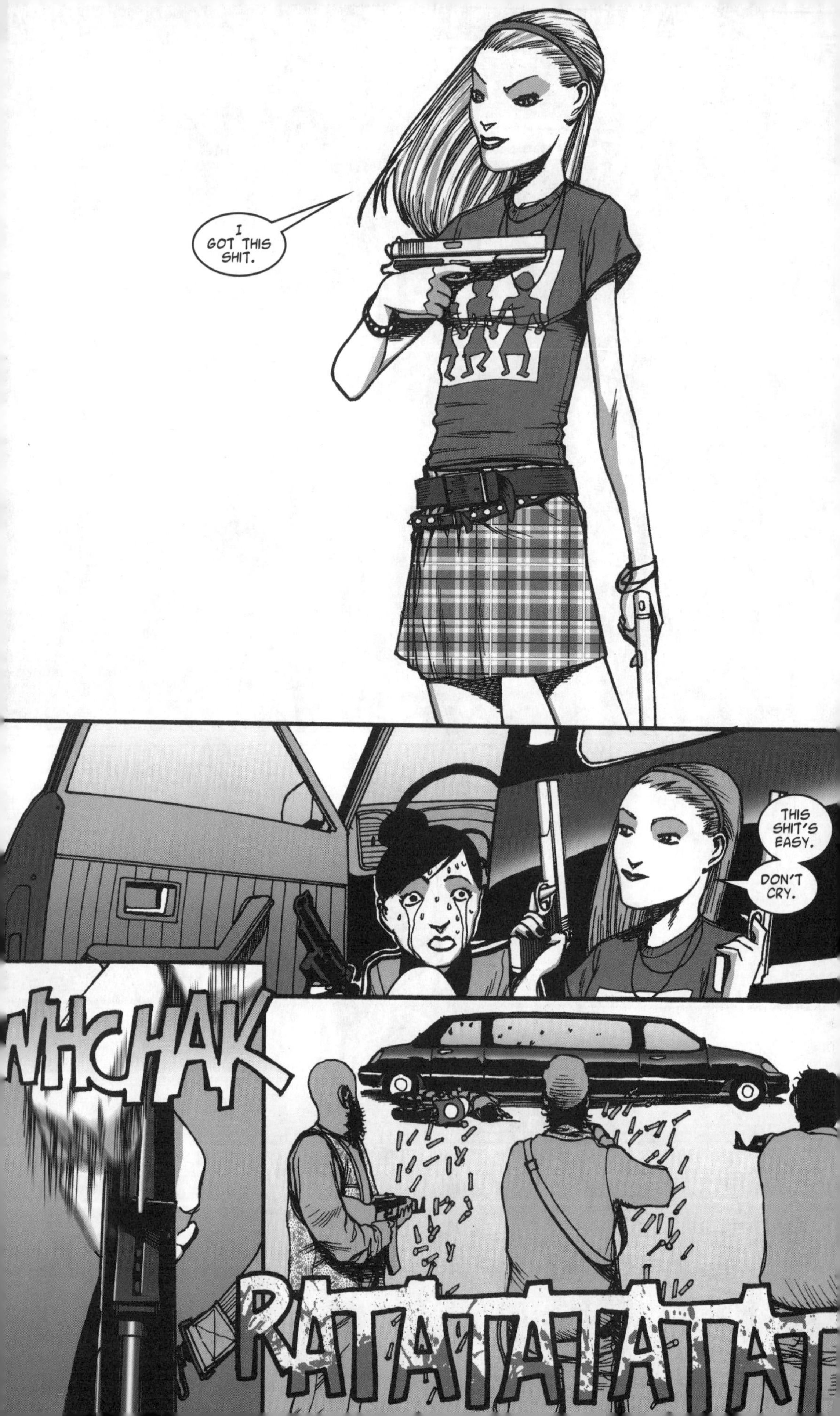
I GOT THIS SHIT.
THIS SHIT'S EASY.
DON'T CRY.
WHCHAK
RATATATATATAT

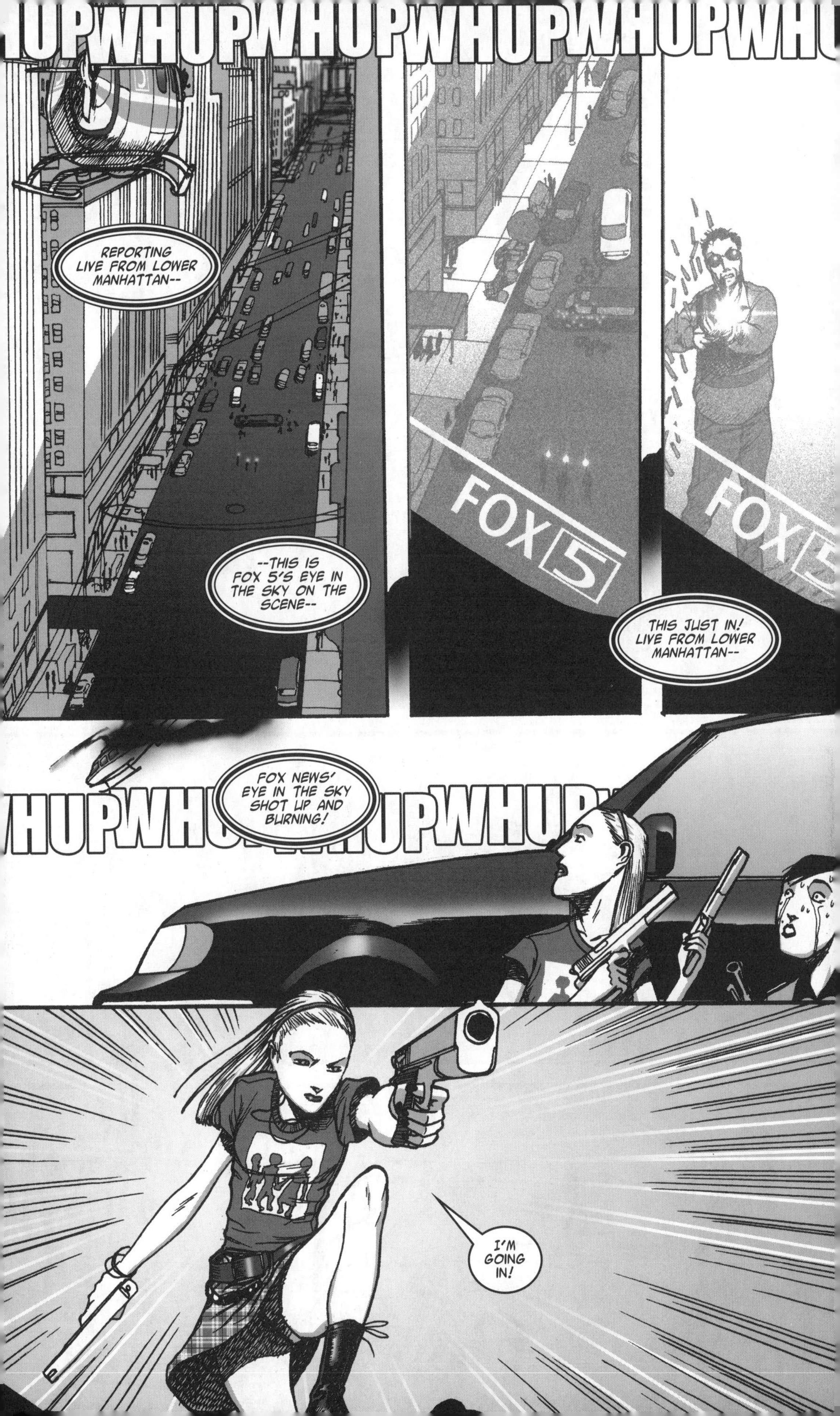
WHUPWHUPWHUPWHUPWHUPWHU
REPORTING LIVE FROM LOWER MANHATTAN--
--THIS IS FOX 5'S EYE IN THE SKY ON THE SCENE--
FOX 5
THIS JUST IN! LIVE FROM LOWER MANHATTAN--
FOX NEWS' EYE IN THE SKY SHOT UP AND BURNING!
WHUPWHUPWHUPWHUP
I'M GOING IN!

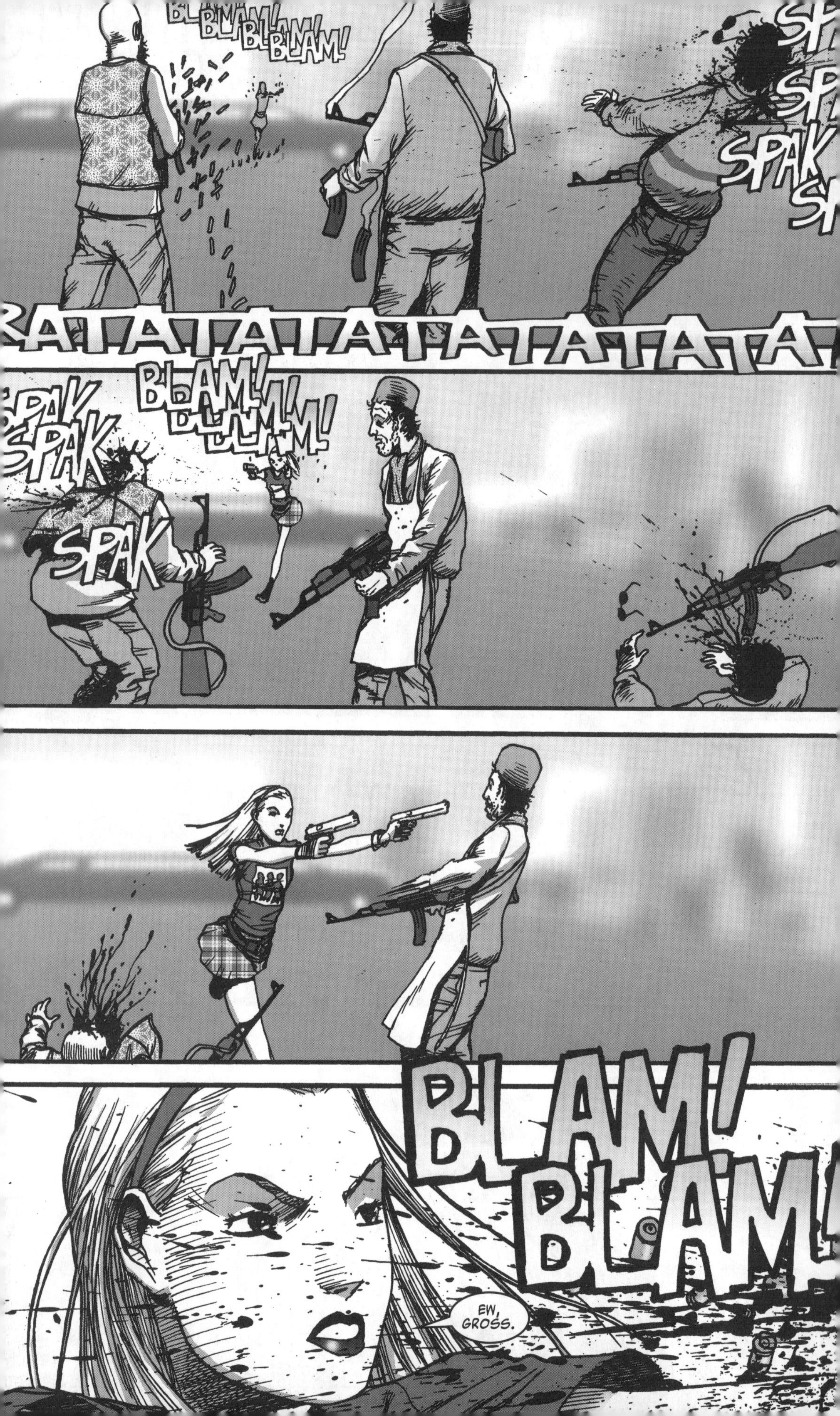
BLAM! BLAM! BLAM! BLAM!
SPAK SPAK SPAK
RATATATATATATATATA
SPAK SPAK
BLAM! BLAM! BLAM!
SPAK
BLAM!
BLAM!
EW, GROSS.

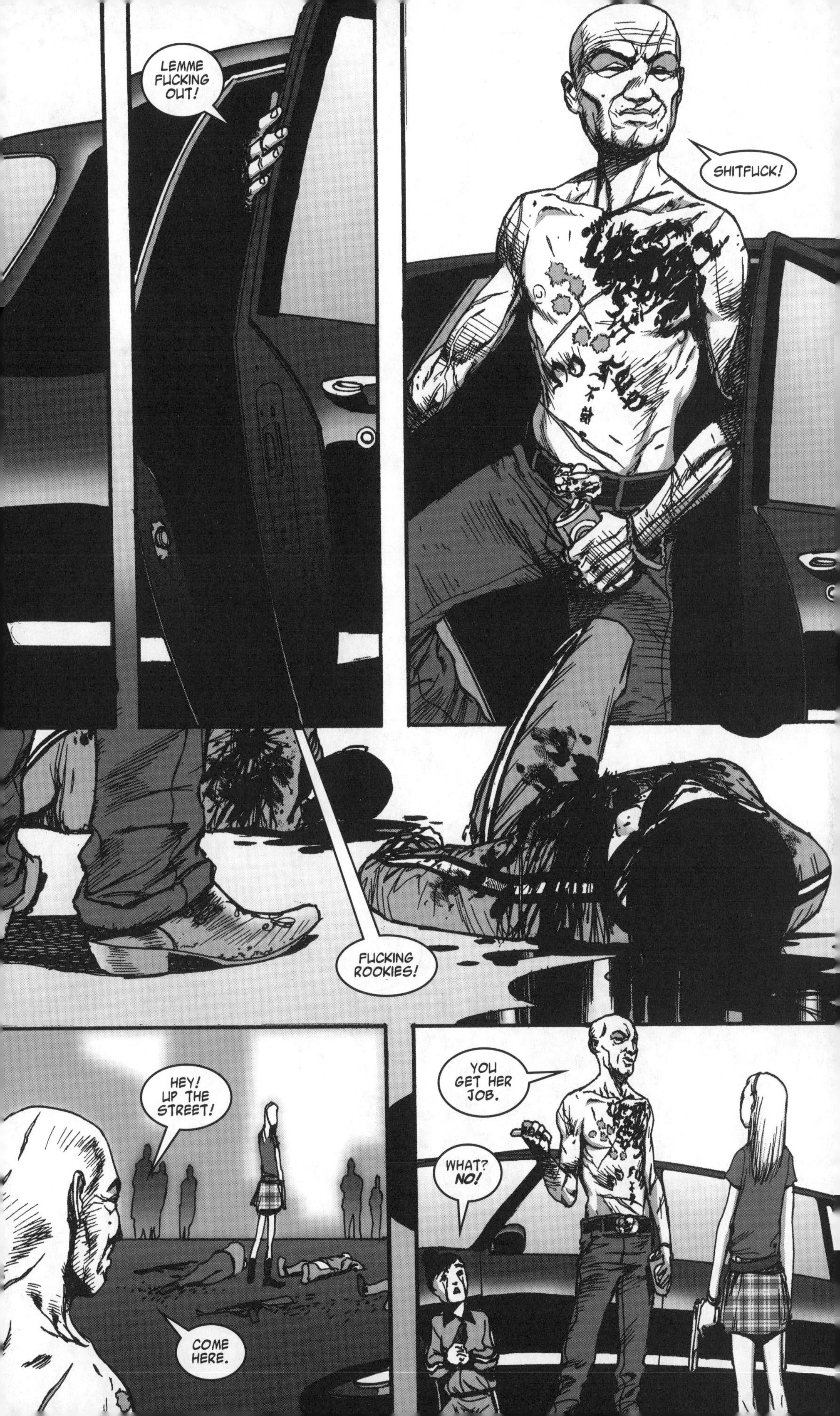
LEMME FUCKING OUT!
SHITFUCK!
FUCKING ROOKIES!
HEY! UP THE STREET!
COME HERE.
YOU GET HER JOB.
WHAT? NO!

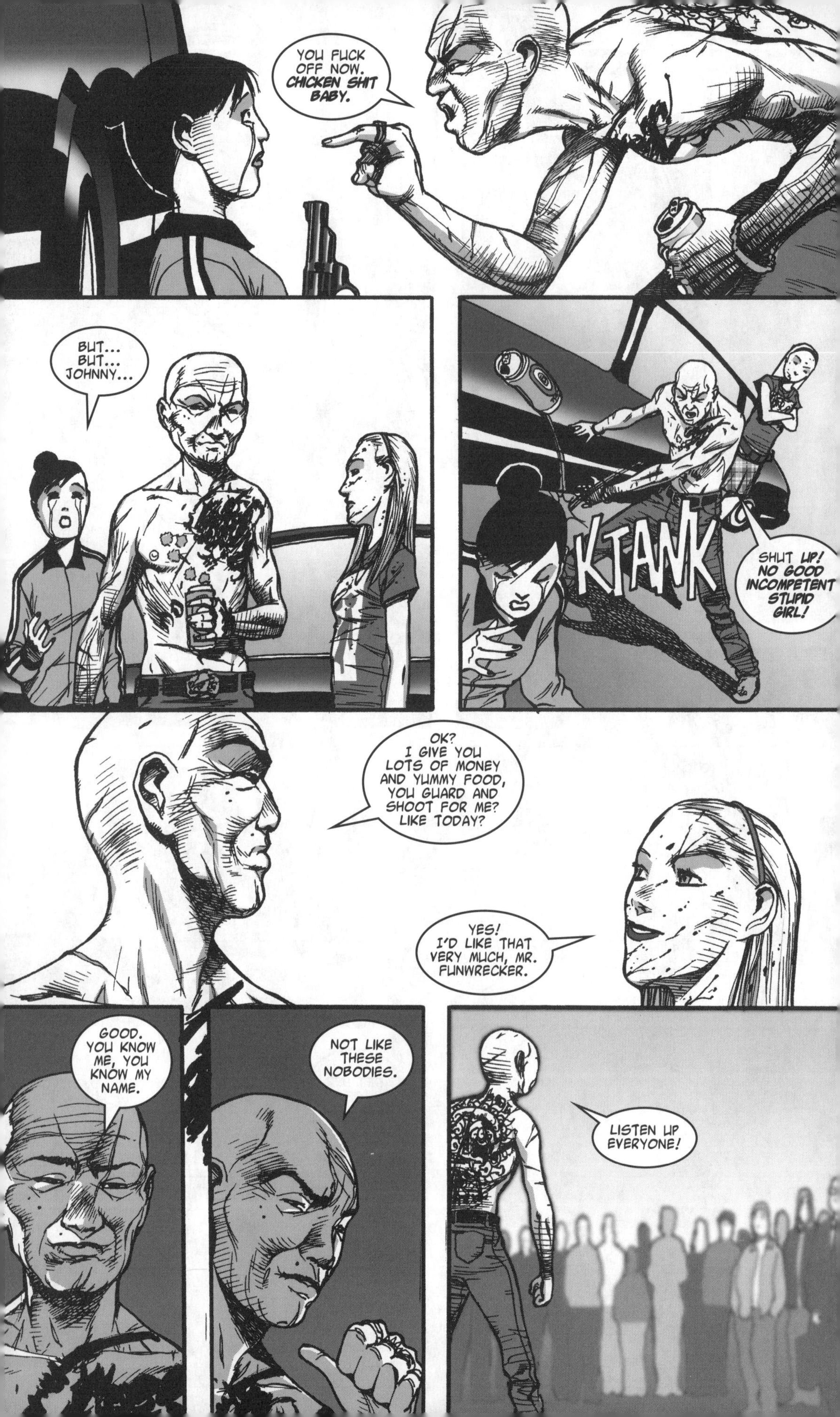
YOU FUCK OFF NOW. CHICKEN SHIT BABY.
BUT... BUT... JOHNNY...
KTANK
SHUT UP! NO GOOD INCOMPETENT STUPID GIRL!
OK? I GIVE YOU LOTS OF MONEY AND YUMMY FOOD, YOU GUARD AND SHOOT FOR ME? LIKE TODAY?
YES! I'D LIKE THAT VERY MUCH, MR. FUNWRECKER.
GOOD. YOU KNOW ME, YOU KNOW MY NAME.
NOT LIKE THESE NOBODIES.
LISTEN UP EVERYONE!

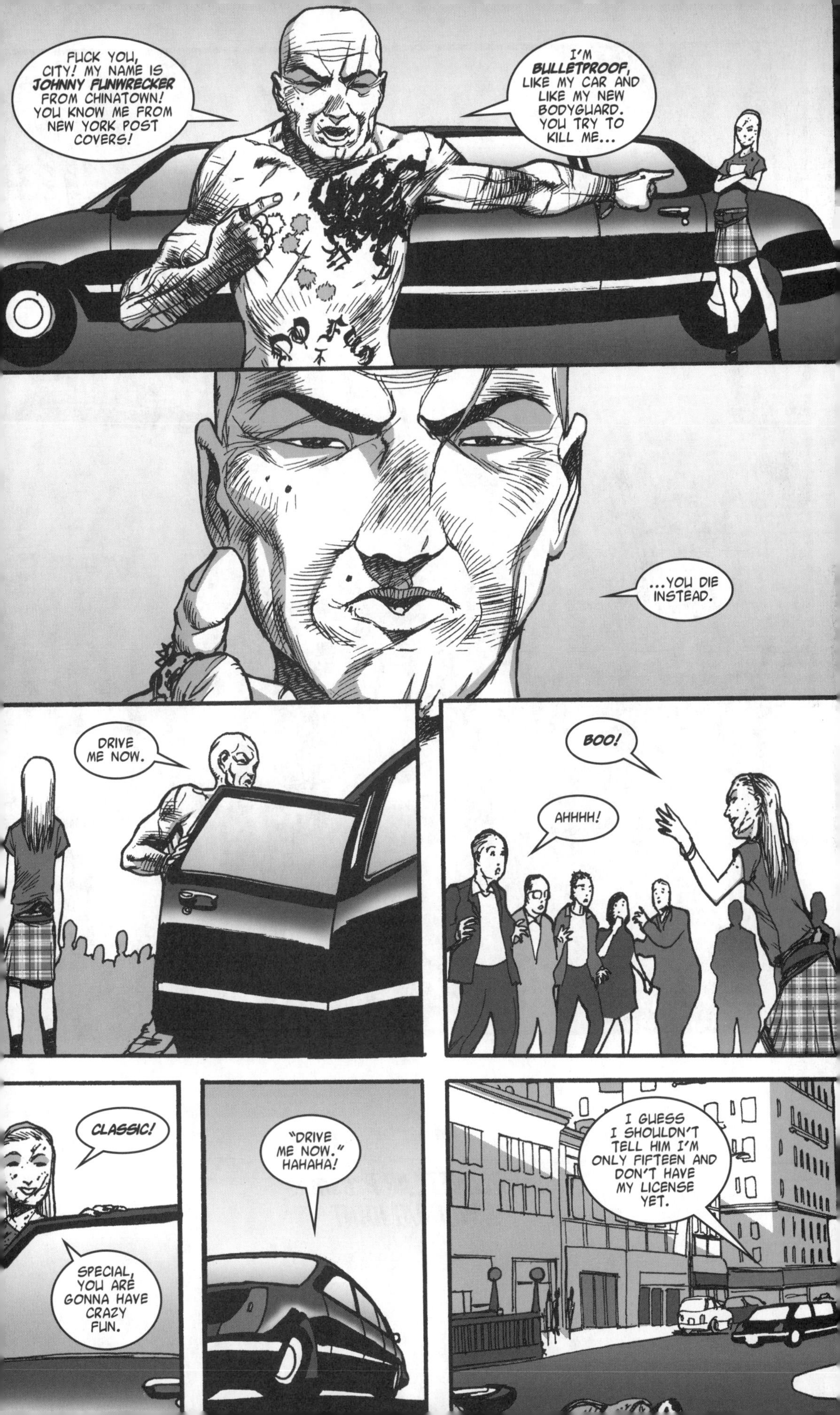
FUCK YOU, CITY! MY NAME IS JOHNNY FLINWRECKER FROM CHINATOWN! YOU KNOW ME FROM NEW YORK POST COVERS!
I'M BULLETPROOF, LIKE MY CAR AND LIKE MY NEW BODYGUARD. YOU TRY TO KILL ME...
...YOU DIE INSTEAD.
DRIVE ME NOW.
BOO!
AHHHH!
CLASSIC!
SPECIAL, YOU ARE GONNA HAVE CRAZY FUN.
"DRIVE ME NOW." HAHAHA!
I GUESS I SHOULDN'T TELL HIM I'M ONLY FIFTEEN AND DON'T HAVE MY LICENSE YET.

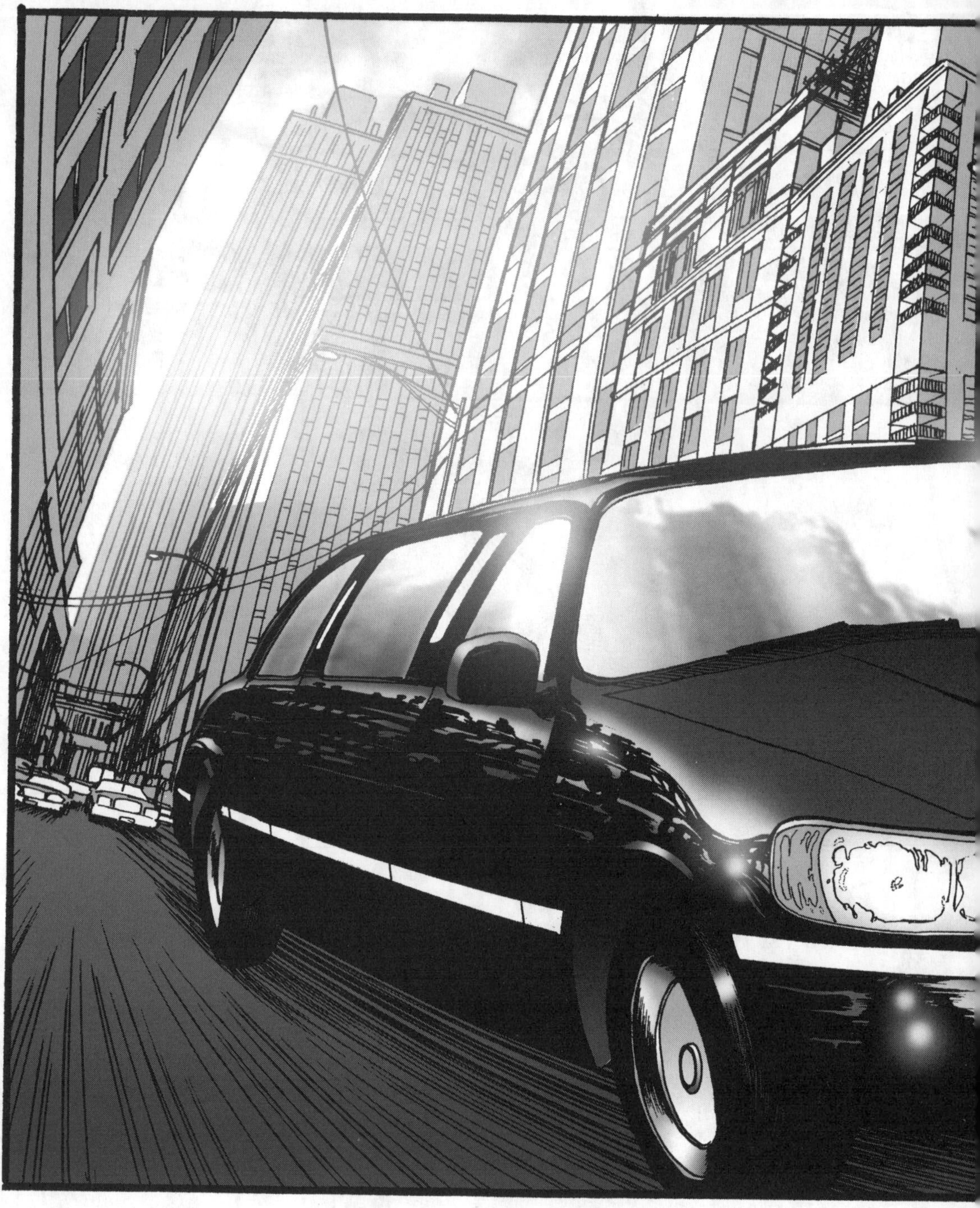

AIT/PLANET LAR Presents
A WOOD/G JOINT

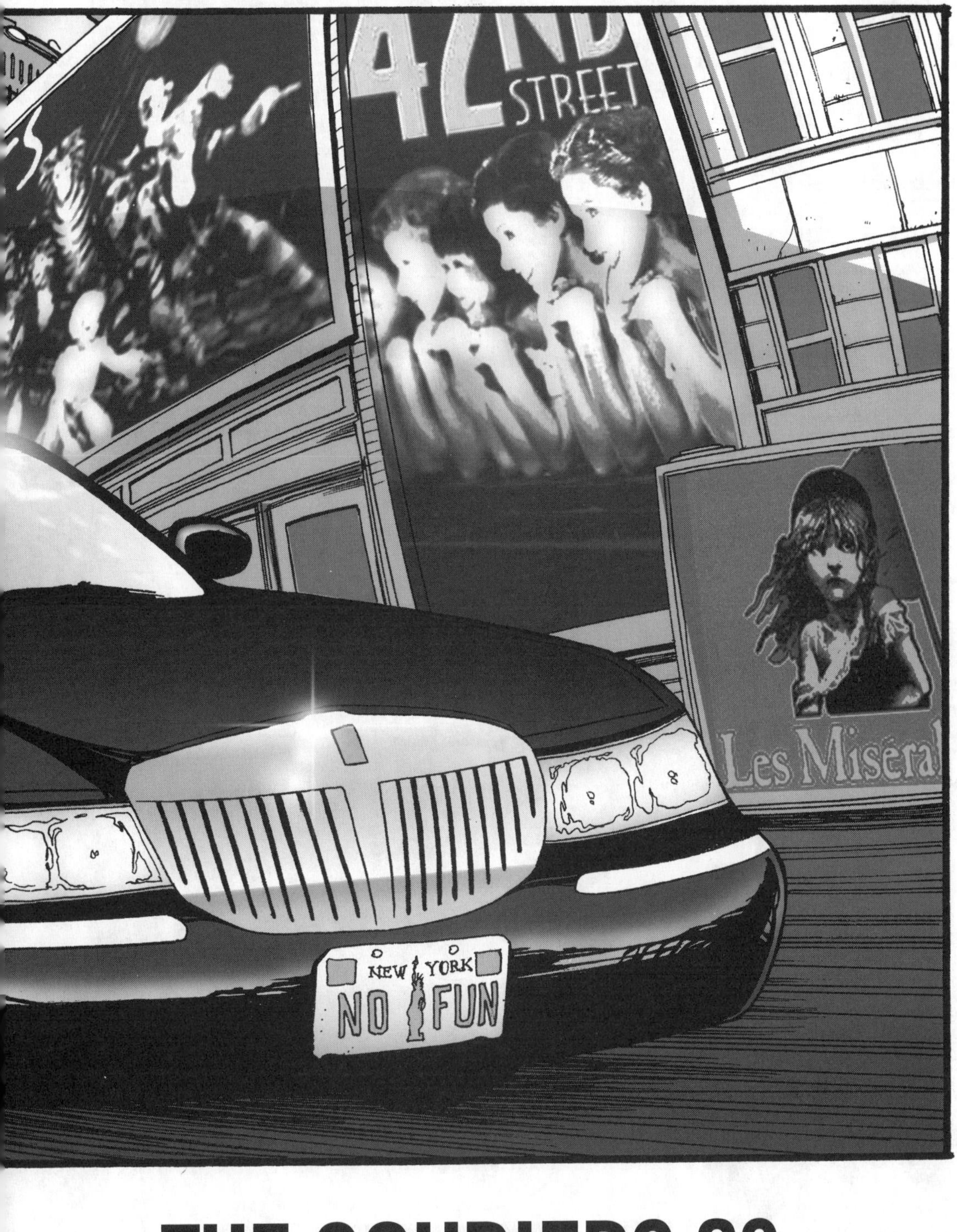
42ND
STREET
Les Miséra
NEW YORK
NO FUN

THE COURIERS 03

THE BALLAD OF JOHNNY FUNWRECKER

Story: **BRIAN WOOD**
Art & SFX: **ROB G**
Lettering: **RYAN YOUNT**

Produced by AIT/PLANET LAR San Francisco

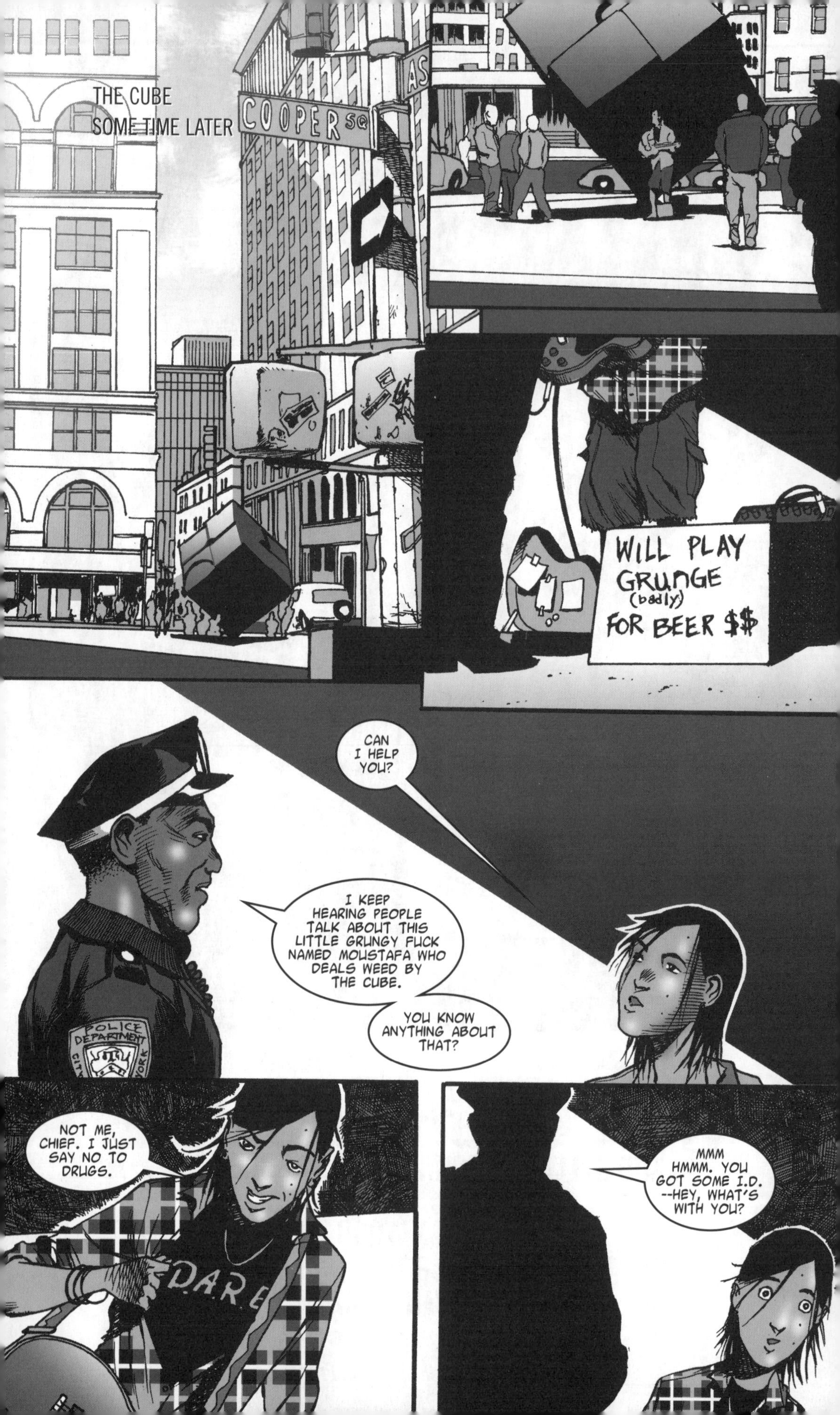
THE CUBE
SOME TIME LATER
COOPER SQ
AS
WILL PLAY GRUNGE (badly) FOR BEER $$
CAN I HELP YOU?
I KEEP HEARING PEOPLE TALK ABOUT THIS LITTLE GRUNGY FUCK NAMED MOUSTAFA WHO DEALS WEED BY THE CUBE.
YOU KNOW ANYTHING ABOUT THAT?
POLICE DEPARTMENT
NOT ME, CHIEF. I JUST SAY NO TO DRUGS.
D.A.R.E
MMM HMMM. YOU GOT SOME I.D. --HEY, WHAT'S WITH YOU?

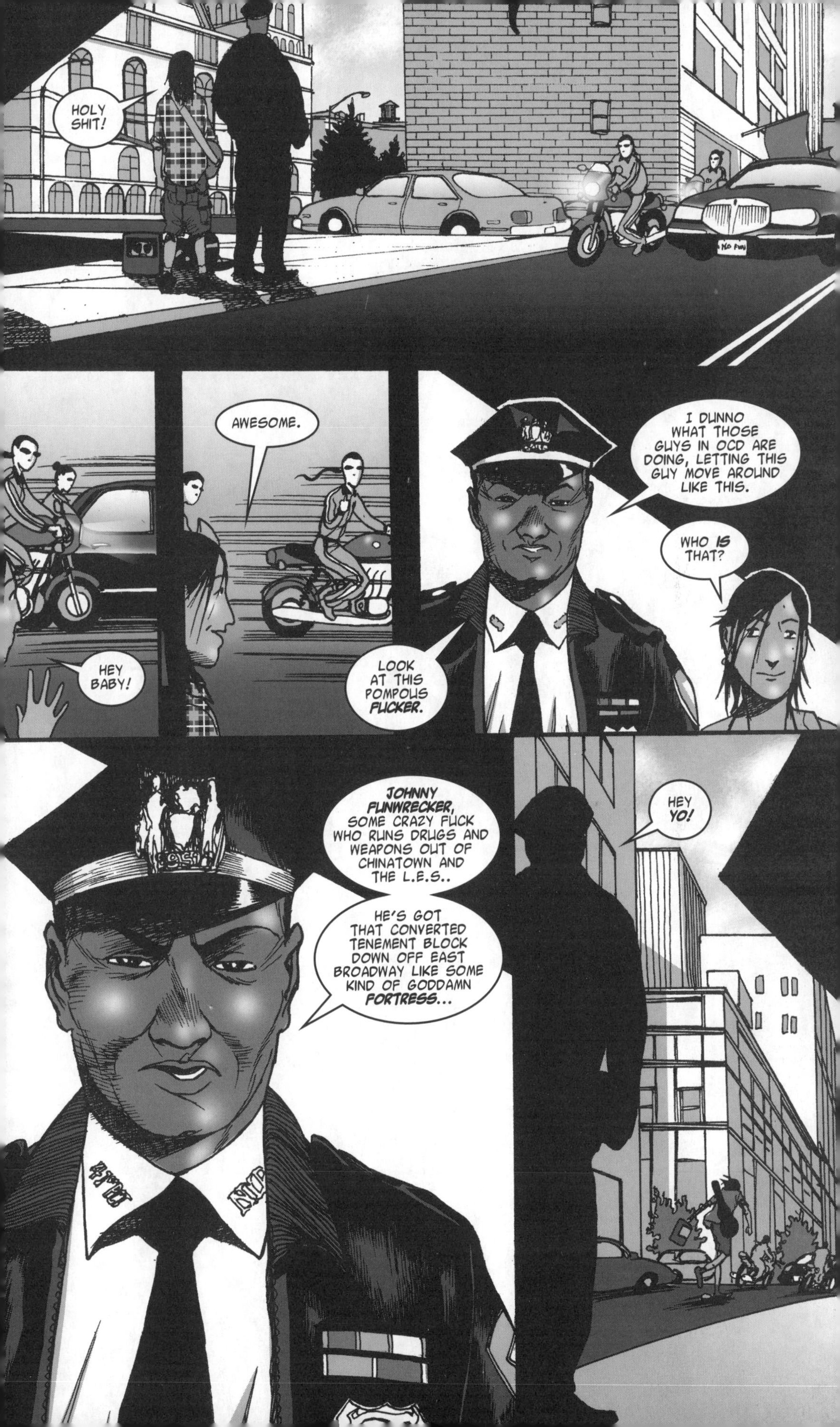
HOLY SHIT!
AWESOME.
HEY BABY!
I DUNNO WHAT THOSE GUYS IN OCD ARE DOING, LETTING THIS GUY MOVE AROUND LIKE THIS.
LOOK AT THIS POMPOUS **FUCKER**.
WHO **IS** THAT?
JOHNNY FUNWRECKER, SOME CRAZY FUCK WHO RUNS DRUGS AND WEAPONS OUT OF CHINATOWN AND THE L.E.S..
HE'S GOT THAT CONVERTED TENEMENT BLOCK DOWN OFF EAST BROADWAY LIKE SOME KIND OF GODDAMN **FORTRESS**...
HEY **YO!**

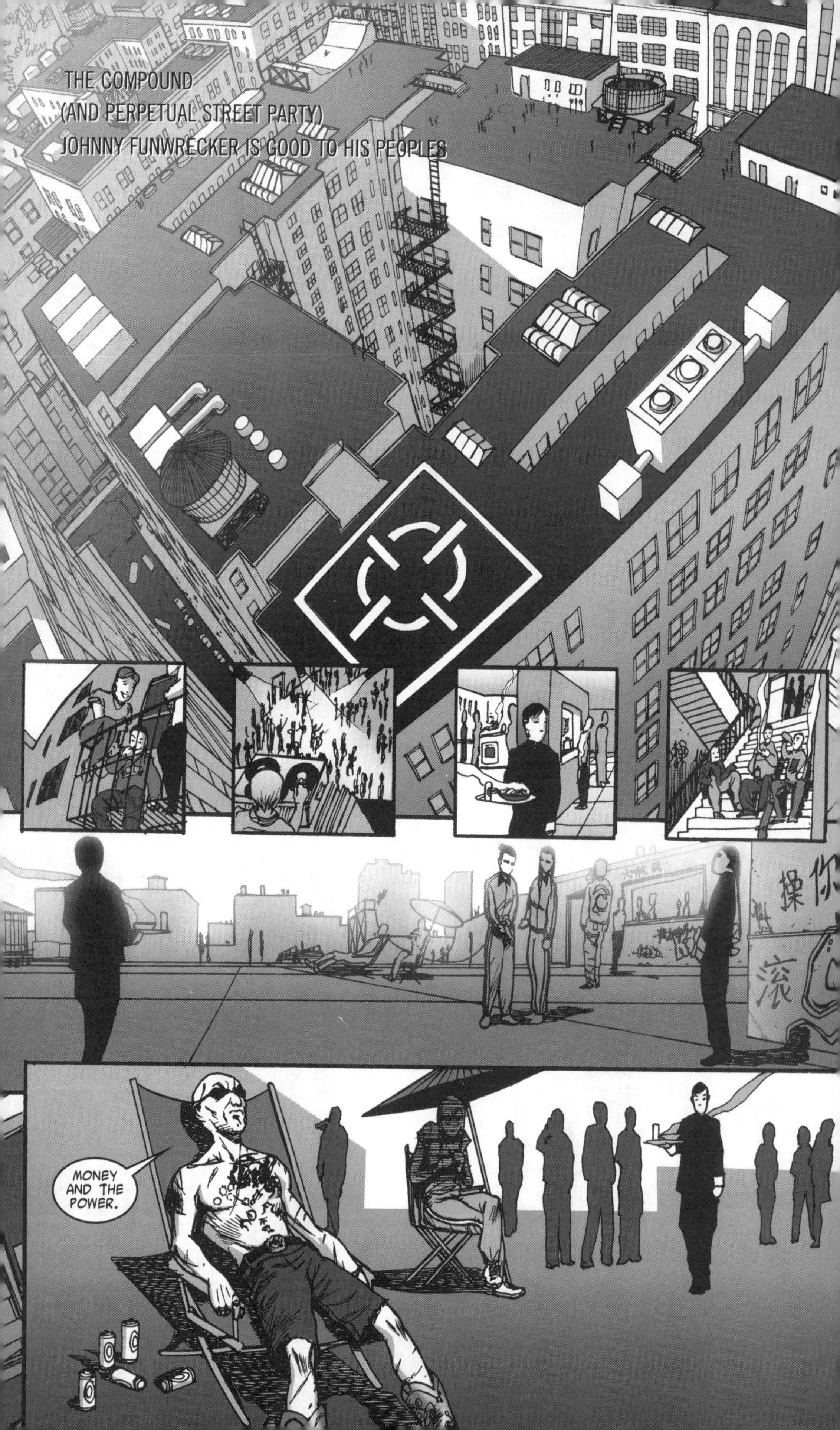
THE COMPOUND
(AND PERPETUAL STREET PARTY)
JOHNNY FUNWRECKER IS GOOD TO HIS PEOPLES
操你
滚
MONEY AND THE POWER.

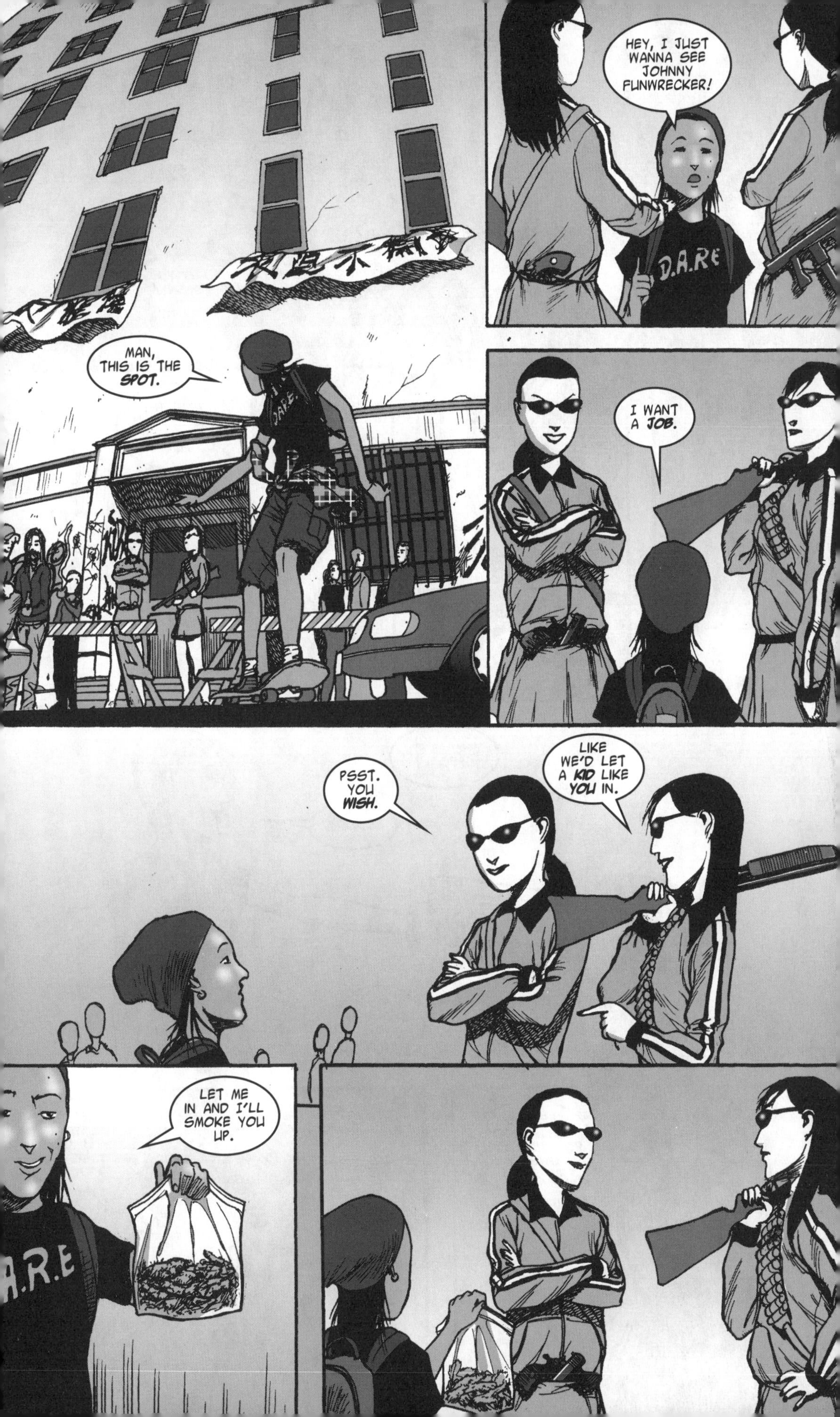
HEY, I JUST WANNA SEE JOHNNY FUNWRECKER!
MAN, THIS IS THE **SPOT**.
I WANT A **JOB**.
PSST. YOU **WISH**.
LIKE WE'D LET A **KID** LIKE **YOU** IN.
LET ME IN AND I'LL SMOKE YOU UP.

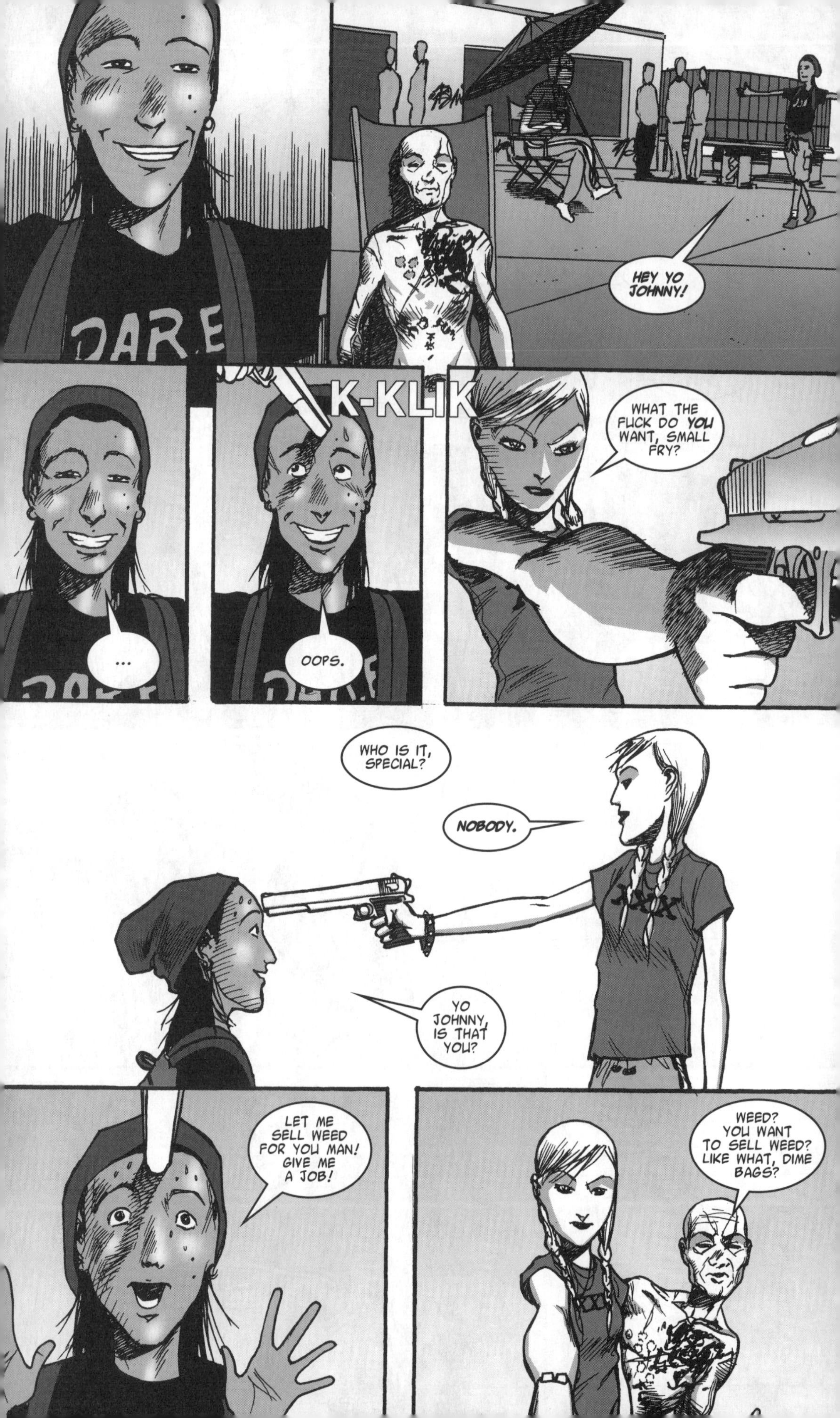
DARE
HEY YO JOHNNY!
...
K-KLIK
OOPS.
WHAT THE FUCK DO YOU WANT, SMALL FRY?
WHO IS IT, SPECIAL?
NOBODY.
YO JOHNNY, IS THAT YOU?
LET ME SELL WEED FOR YOU MAN! GIVE ME A JOB!
WEED? YOU WANT TO SELL WEED? LIKE WHAT, DIME BAGS?

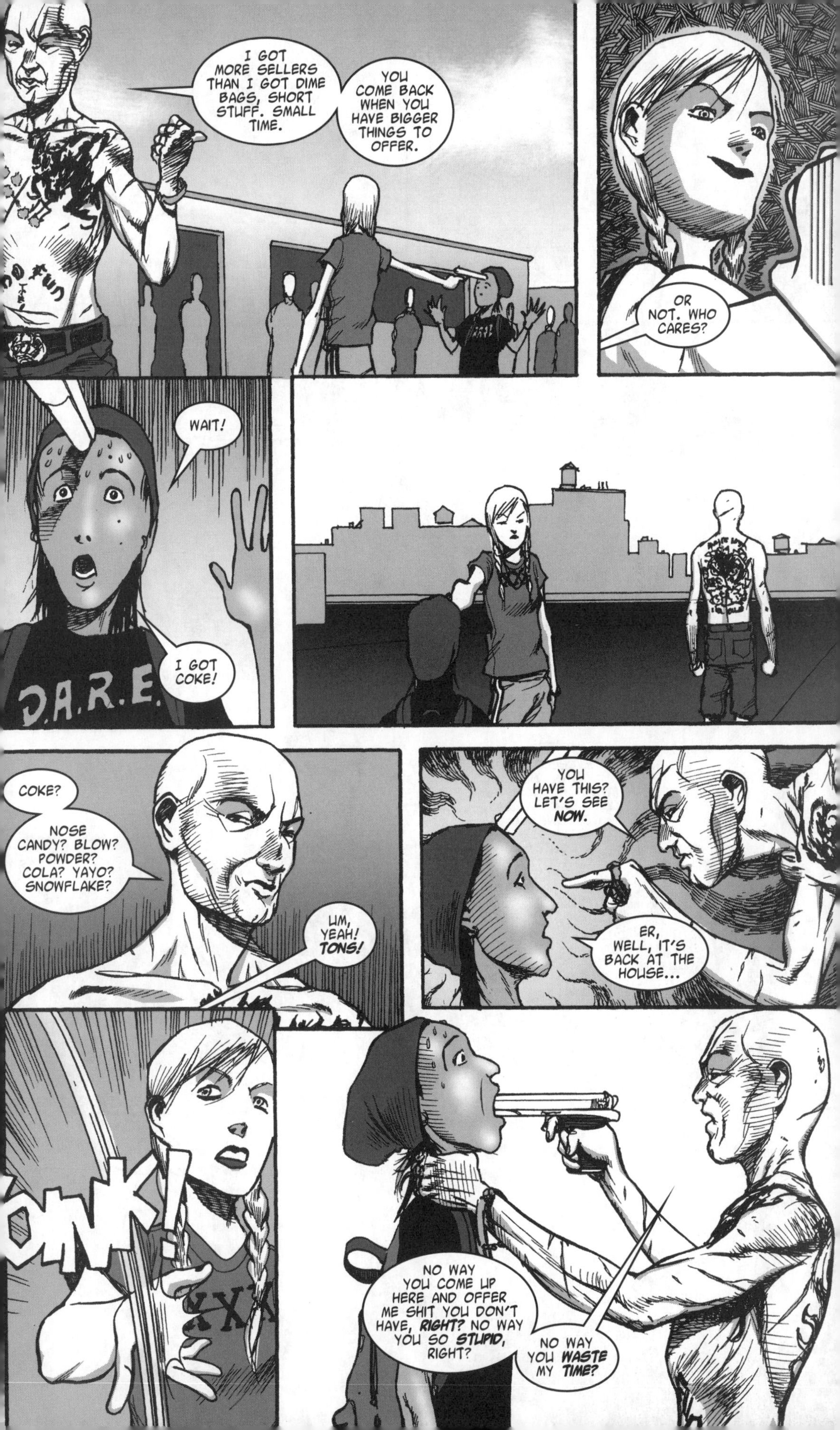
I GOT MORE SELLERS THAN I GOT DIME BAGS, SHORT STUFF. SMALL TIME.
YOU COME BACK WHEN YOU HAVE BIGGER THINGS TO OFFER.
OR NOT. WHO CARES?
WAIT!
I GOT COKE!
D.A.R.E.
COKE?
NOSE CANDY? BLOW? POWDER? COLA? YAYO? SNOWFLAKE?
UM, YEAH! TONS!
YOU HAVE THIS? LET'S SEE NOW.
ER, WELL, IT'S BACK AT THE HOUSE...
NO WAY YOU COME UP HERE AND OFFER ME SHIT YOU DON'T HAVE, RIGHT? NO WAY YOU SO STUPID, RIGHT?
NO WAY YOU WASTE MY TIME?

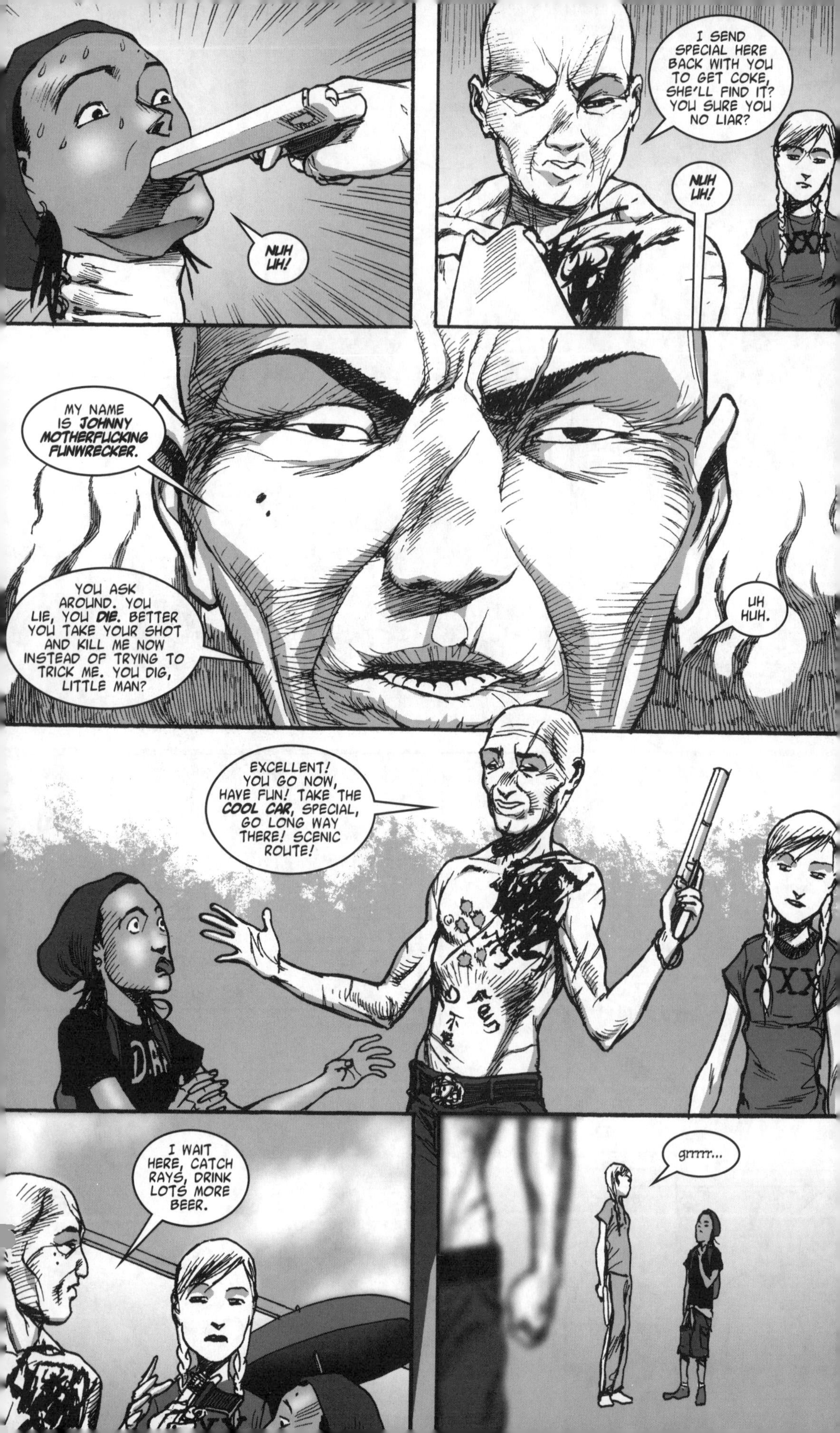
NUH UH!
I SEND SPECIAL HERE BACK WITH YOU TO GET COKE, SHE'LL FIND IT? YOU SURE YOU NO LIAR?
NUH UH!
MY NAME IS JOHNNY MOTHERFUCKING FUNWRECKER.
YOU ASK AROUND. YOU LIE, YOU DIE. BETTER YOU TAKE YOUR SHOT AND KILL ME NOW INSTEAD OF TRYING TO TRICK ME. YOU DIG, LITTLE MAN?
UH HUH.
EXCELLENT! YOU GO NOW, HAVE FUN! TAKE THE COOL CAR, SPECIAL, GO LONG WAY THERE! SCENIC ROUTE!
I WAIT HERE, CATCH RAYS, DRINK LOTS MORE BEER.
grrrrr...

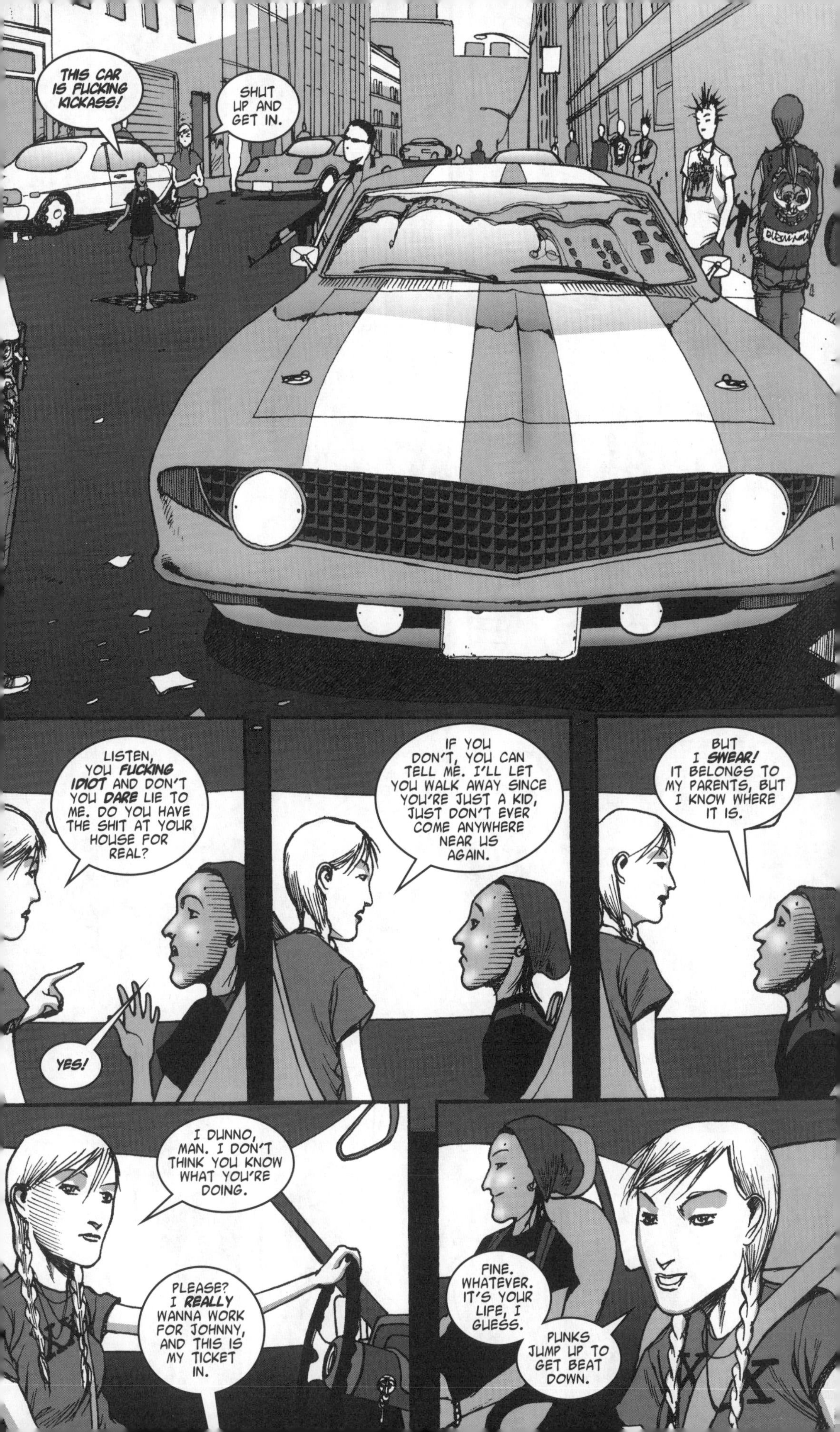
THIS CAR IS FUCKING KICKASS!
SHUT UP AND GET IN.
LISTEN, YOU FUCKING IDIOT AND DON'T YOU DARE LIE TO ME. DO YOU HAVE THE SHIT AT YOUR HOUSE FOR REAL?
YES!
IF YOU DON'T, YOU CAN TELL ME. I'LL LET YOU WALK AWAY SINCE YOU'RE JUST A KID, JUST DON'T EVER COME ANYWHERE NEAR US AGAIN.
BUT I SWEAR! IT BELONGS TO MY PARENTS, BUT I KNOW WHERE IT IS.
I DUNNO, MAN. I DON'T THINK YOU KNOW WHAT YOU'RE DOING.
PLEASE? I REALLY WANNA WORK FOR JOHNNY, AND THIS IS MY TICKET IN.
FINE. WHATEVER. IT'S YOUR LIFE, I GUESS.
PUNKS JUMP UP TO GET BEAT DOWN.

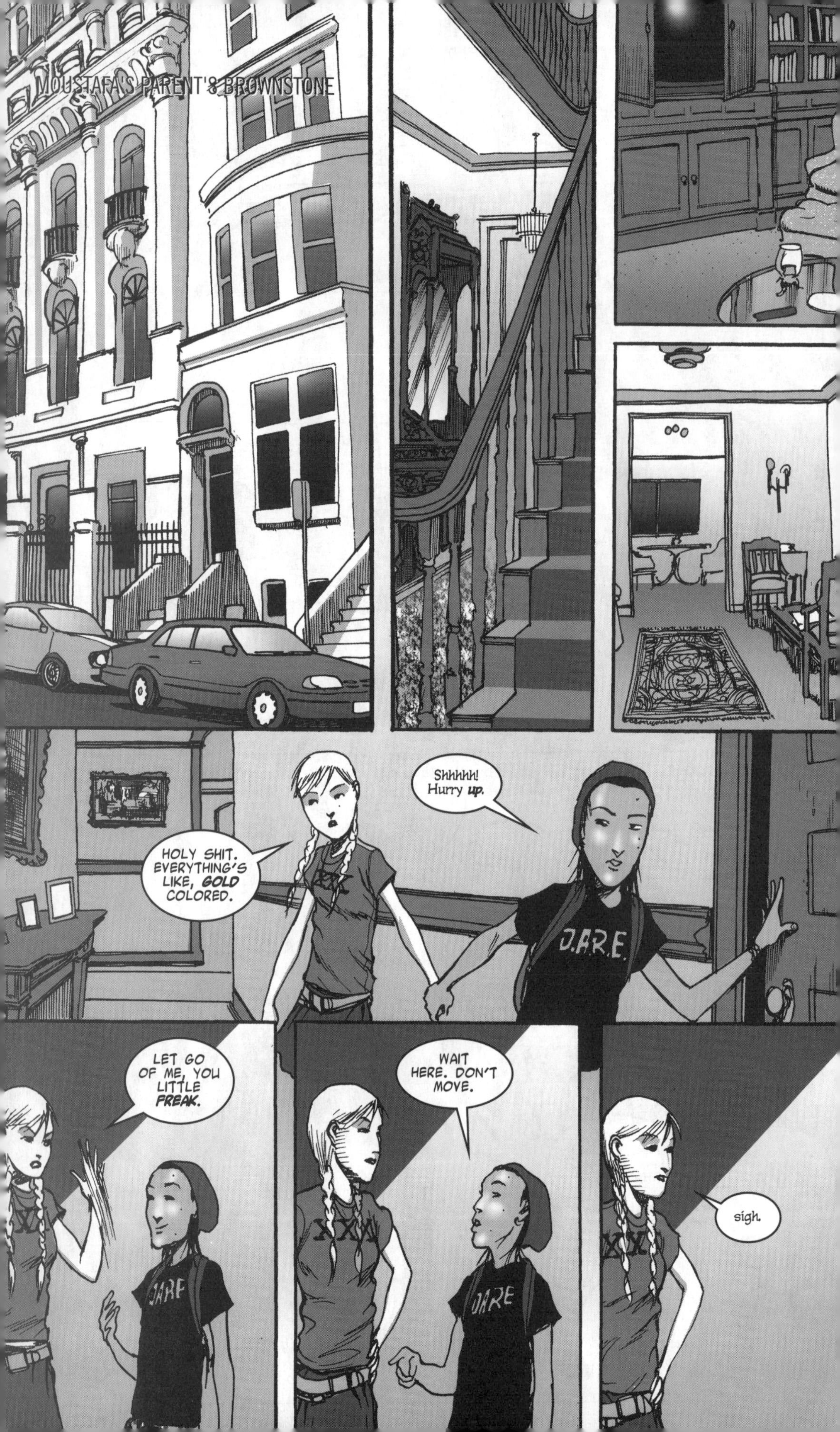
MOUSTAFA'S PARENT'S BROWNSTONE
Shhhhh! Hurry up.
HOLY SHIT. EVERYTHING'S LIKE, GOLD COLORED.
D.A.R.E.
LET GO OF ME, YOU LITTLE FREAK.
WAIT HERE. DON'T MOVE.
sigh.

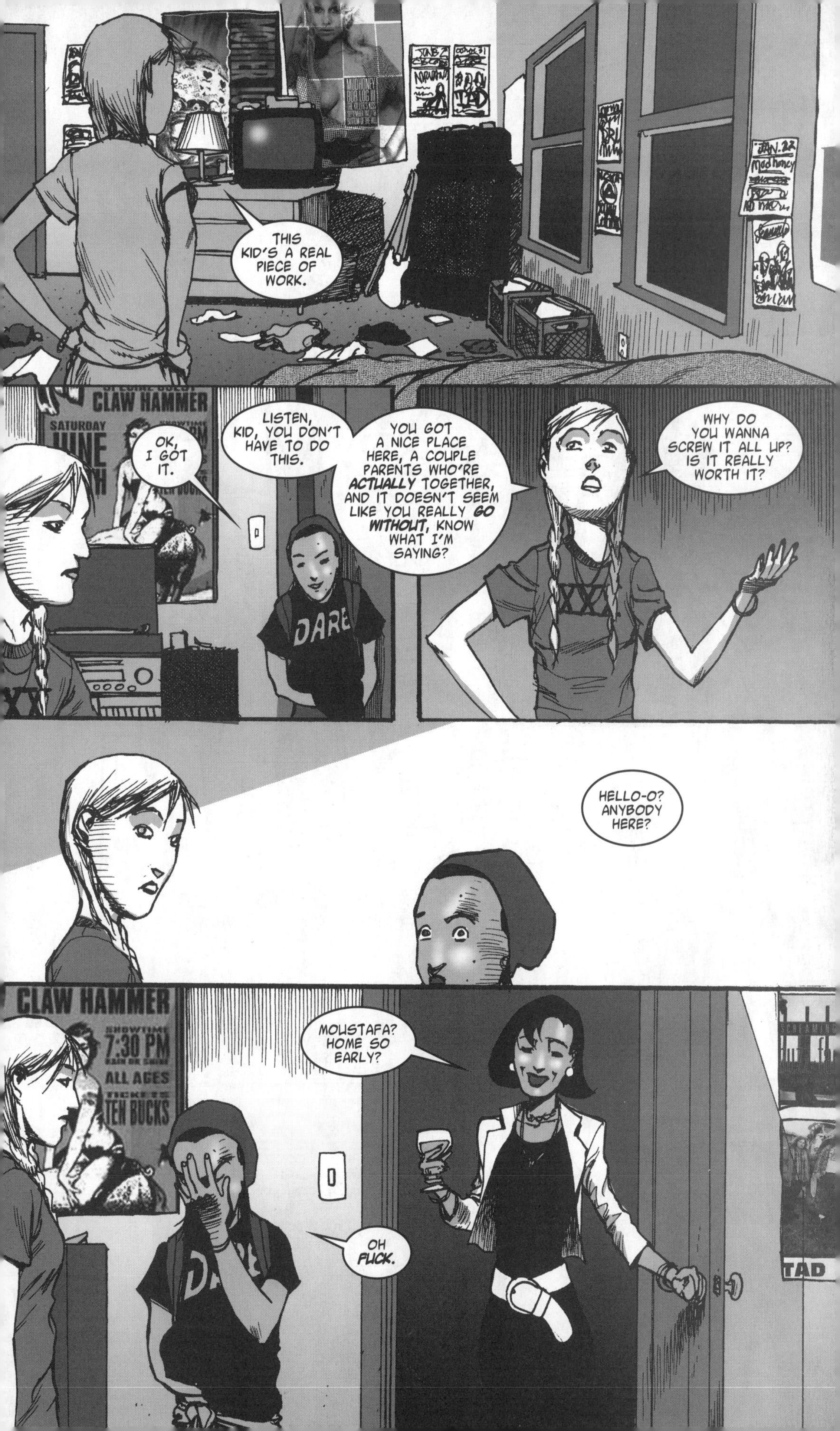
MUDHONEY
THIS KID'S A REAL PIECE OF WORK.
CLAW HAMMER
SATURDAY
OK, I GOT IT.
LISTEN, KID, YOU DON'T HAVE TO DO THIS.
DARE
YOU GOT A NICE PLACE HERE, A COUPLE PARENTS WHO'RE **ACTUALLY** TOGETHER, AND IT DOESN'T SEEM LIKE YOU REALLY **GO WITHOUT**, KNOW WHAT I'M SAYING?
WHY DO YOU WANNA SCREW IT ALL UP? IS IT REALLY WORTH IT?
HELLO-O? ANYBODY HERE?
CLAW HAMMER
SHOWTIME 7:30 PM
ALL AGES
TICKETS TEN BUCKS
MOUSTAFA? HOME SO EARLY?
OH **FUCK**.
TAD

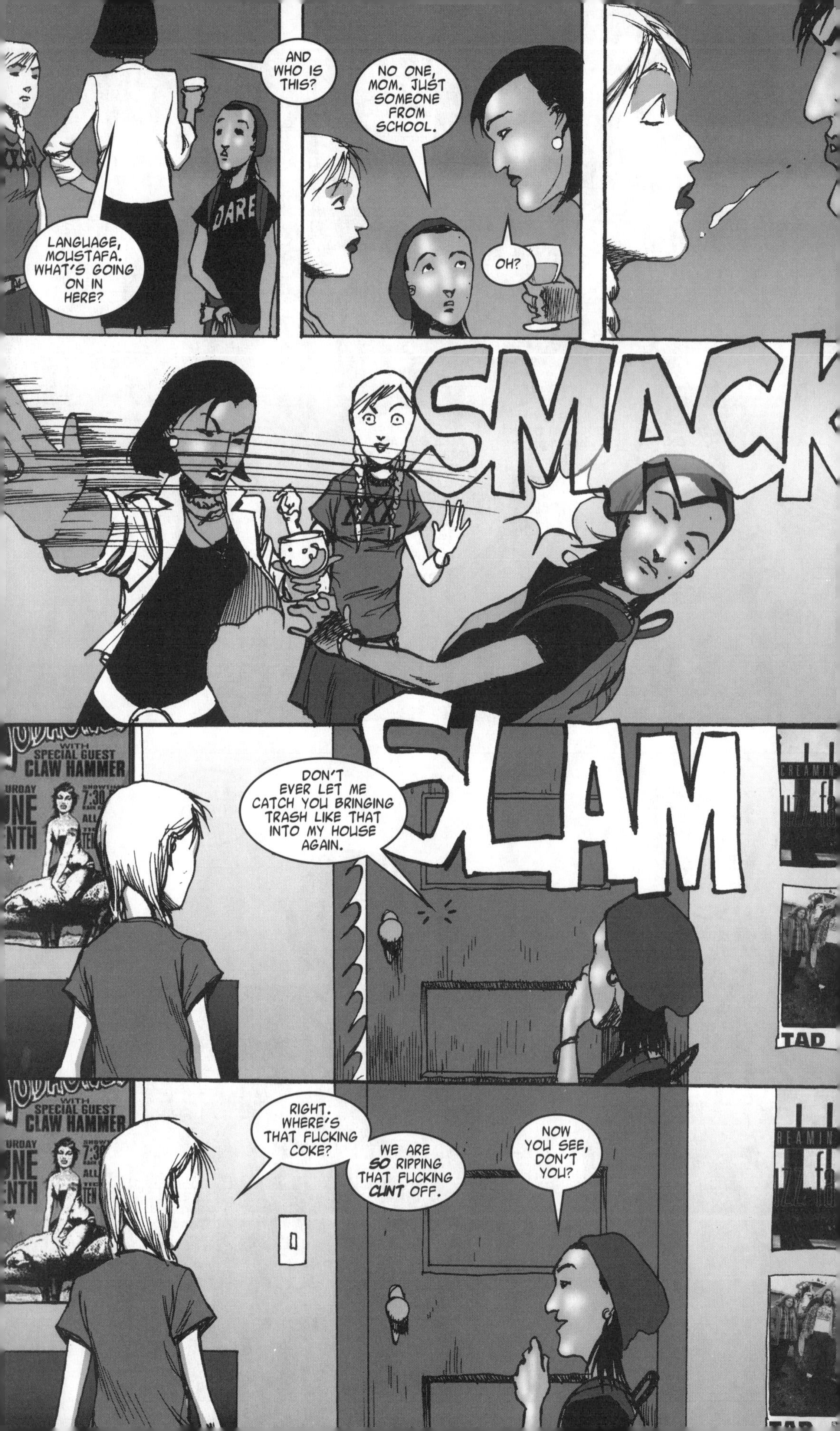

DARE
LANGUAGE, MOUSTAFA. WHAT'S GOING ON IN HERE?
AND WHO IS THIS?
NO ONE, MOM. JUST SOMEONE FROM SCHOOL.
OH?
SMACK
WITH SPECIAL GUEST CLAW HAMMER
SLAM
DON'T EVER LET ME CATCH YOU BRINGING TRASH LIKE THAT INTO MY HOUSE AGAIN.
TAD
WITH SPECIAL GUEST CLAW HAMMER
RIGHT. WHERE'S THAT FUCKING COKE?
WE ARE *SO* RIPPING THAT FUCKING *CUNT* OFF.
NOW YOU SEE, DON'T YOU?

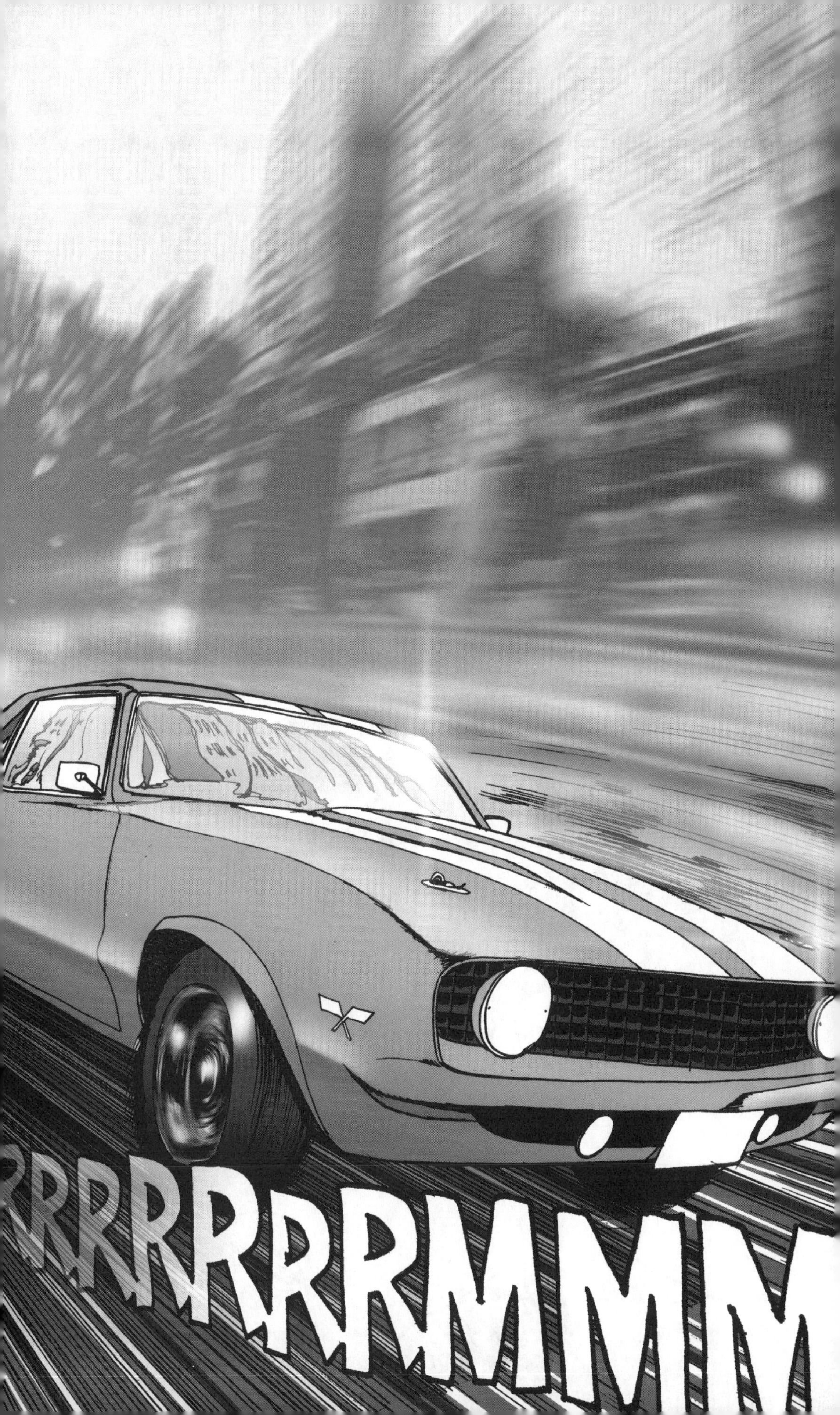
RRRRRRMMMM

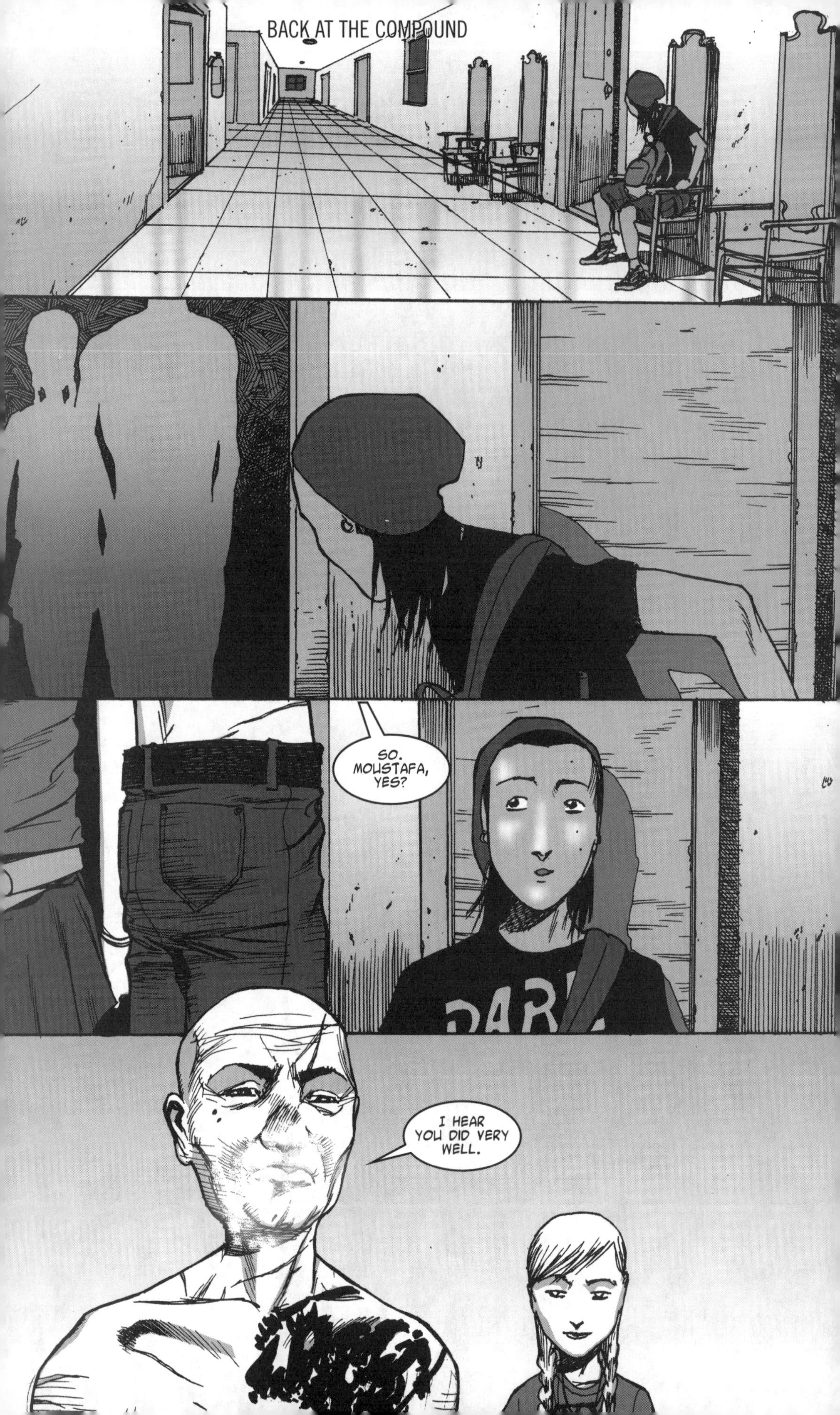
BACK AT THE COMPOUND
SO. MOUSTAFA, YES?
I HEAR YOU DID VERY WELL.

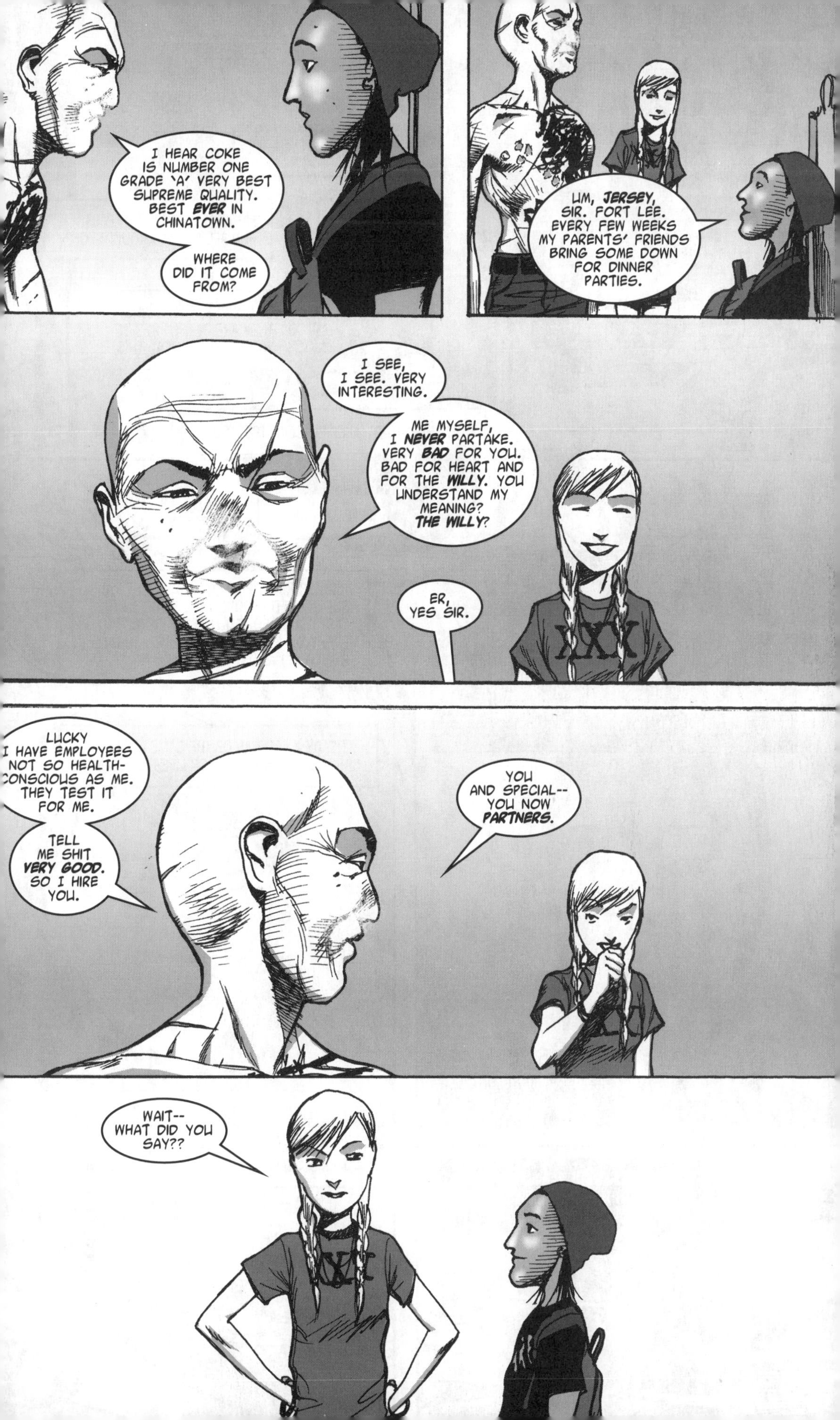

I HEAR COKE IS NUMBER ONE GRADE 'A' VERY BEST SUPREME QUALITY. BEST EVER IN CHINATOWN.
WHERE DID IT COME FROM?
UM, JERSEY, SIR. FORT LEE. EVERY FEW WEEKS MY PARENTS' FRIENDS BRING SOME DOWN FOR DINNER PARTIES.
I SEE, I SEE. VERY INTERESTING.
ME MYSELF, I NEVER PARTAKE. VERY BAD FOR YOU. BAD FOR HEART AND FOR THE WILLY. YOU UNDERSTAND MY MEANING? THE WILLY?
ER, YES SIR.
LUCKY I HAVE EMPLOYEES NOT SO HEALTH-CONSCIOUS AS ME. THEY TEST IT FOR ME.
TELL ME SHIT VERY GOOD. SO I HIRE YOU.
YOU AND SPECIAL-- YOU NOW PARTNERS.
WAIT-- WHAT DID YOU SAY??

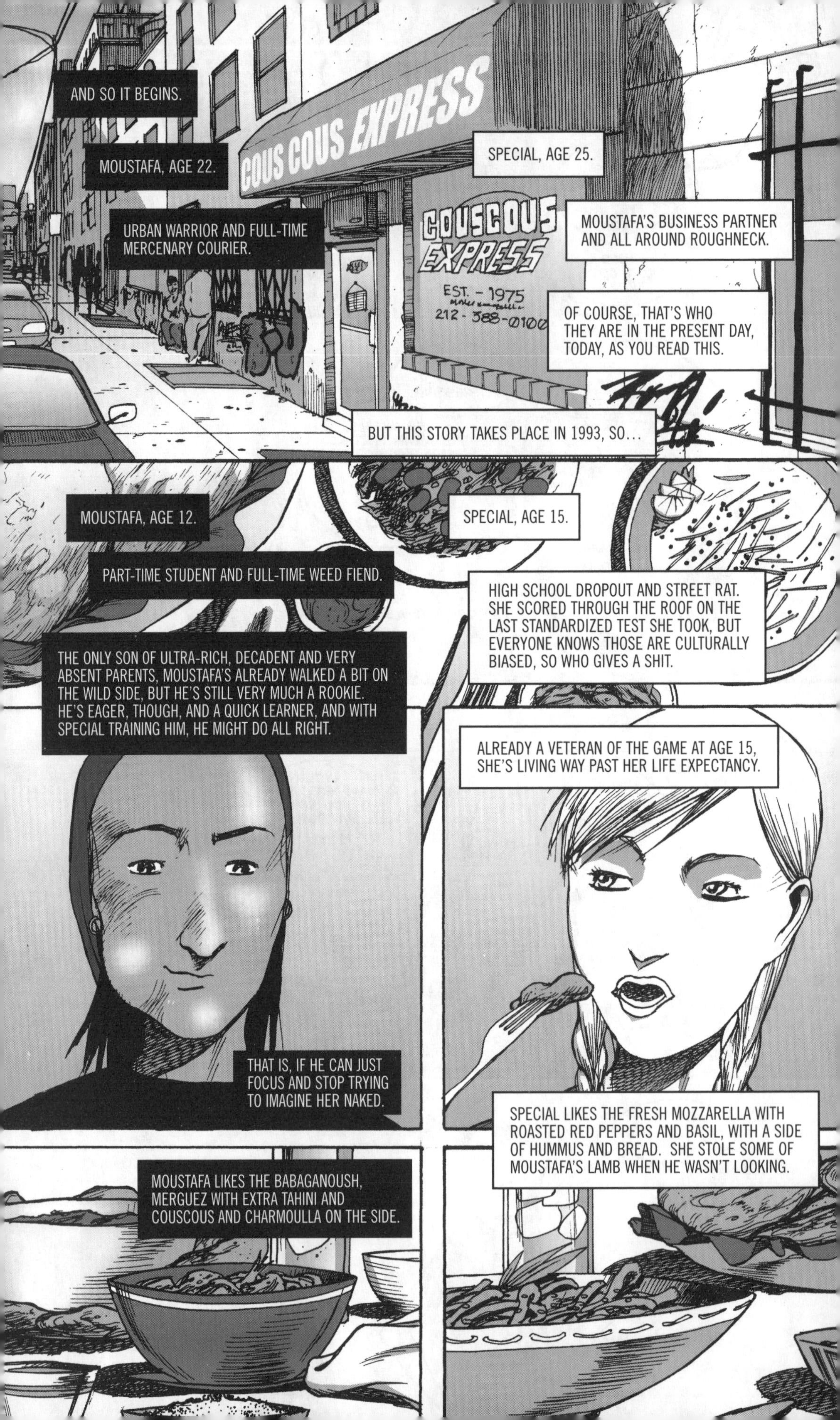
AND SO IT BEGINS.
MOUSTAFA, AGE 22.
URBAN WARRIOR AND FULL-TIME MERCENARY COURIER.
COUS COUS EXPRESS
SPECIAL, AGE 25.
COUSCOUS EXPRESS
EST. - 1975
212 - 388-0100
MOUSTAFA'S BUSINESS PARTNER AND ALL AROUND ROUGHNECK.
OF COURSE, THAT'S WHO THEY ARE IN THE PRESENT DAY, TODAY, AS YOU READ THIS.
BUT THIS STORY TAKES PLACE IN 1993, SO...
MOUSTAFA, AGE 12.
PART-TIME STUDENT AND FULL-TIME WEED FIEND.
THE ONLY SON OF ULTRA-RICH, DECADENT AND VERY ABSENT PARENTS, MOUSTAFA'S ALREADY WALKED A BIT ON THE WILD SIDE, BUT HE'S STILL VERY MUCH A ROOKIE. HE'S EAGER, THOUGH, AND A QUICK LEARNER, AND WITH SPECIAL TRAINING HIM, HE MIGHT DO ALL RIGHT.
SPECIAL, AGE 15.
HIGH SCHOOL DROPOUT AND STREET RAT. SHE SCORED THROUGH THE ROOF ON THE LAST STANDARDIZED TEST SHE TOOK, BUT EVERYONE KNOWS THOSE ARE CULTURALLY BIASED, SO WHO GIVES A SHIT.
THAT IS, IF HE CAN JUST FOCUS AND STOP TRYING TO IMAGINE HER NAKED.
ALREADY A VETERAN OF THE GAME AT AGE 15, SHE'S LIVING WAY PAST HER LIFE EXPECTANCY.
MOUSTAFA LIKES THE BABAGANOUSH, MERGUEZ WITH EXTRA TAHINI AND COUSCOUS AND CHARMOULLA ON THE SIDE.
SPECIAL LIKES THE FRESH MOZZARELLA WITH ROASTED RED PEPPERS AND BASIL, WITH A SIDE OF HUMMUS AND BREAD. SHE STOLE SOME OF MOUSTAFA'S LAMB WHEN HE WASN'T LOOKING.

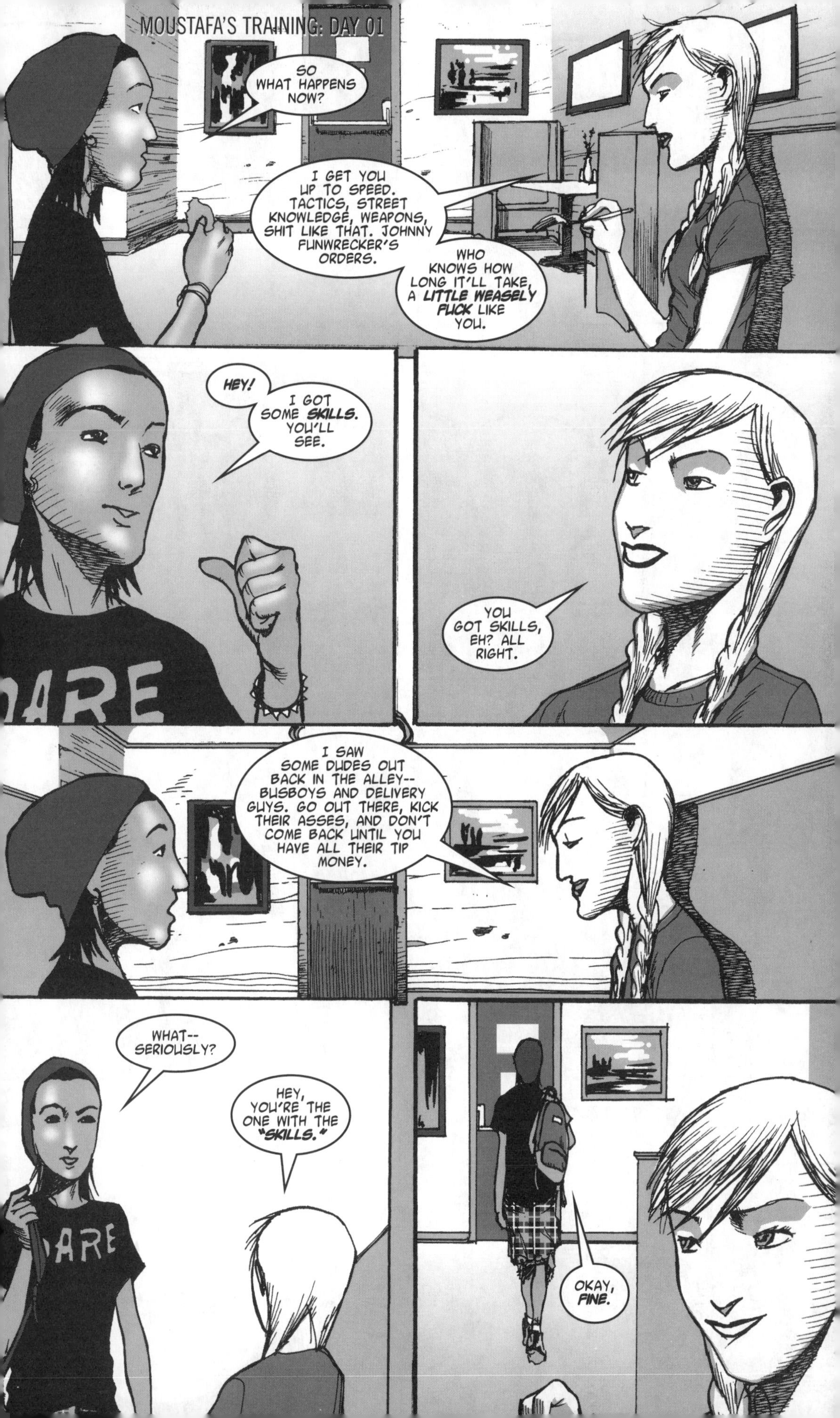
MOUSTAFA'S TRAINING: DAY 01
SO WHAT HAPPENS NOW?
I GET YOU UP TO SPEED. TACTICS, STREET KNOWLEDGE, WEAPONS, SHIT LIKE THAT. JOHNNY FUNWRECKER'S ORDERS.
WHO KNOWS HOW LONG IT'LL TAKE, A LITTLE WEASELY FUCK LIKE YOU.
HEY!
I GOT SOME SKILLS. YOU'LL SEE.
YOU GOT SKILLS, EH? ALL RIGHT.
I SAW SOME DUDES OUT BACK IN THE ALLEY-- BUSBOYS AND DELIVERY GUYS. GO OUT THERE, KICK THEIR ASSES, AND DON'T COME BACK UNTIL YOU HAVE ALL THEIR TIP MONEY.
WHAT-- SERIOUSLY?
HEY, YOU'RE THE ONE WITH THE "SKILLS."
OKAY, FINE.

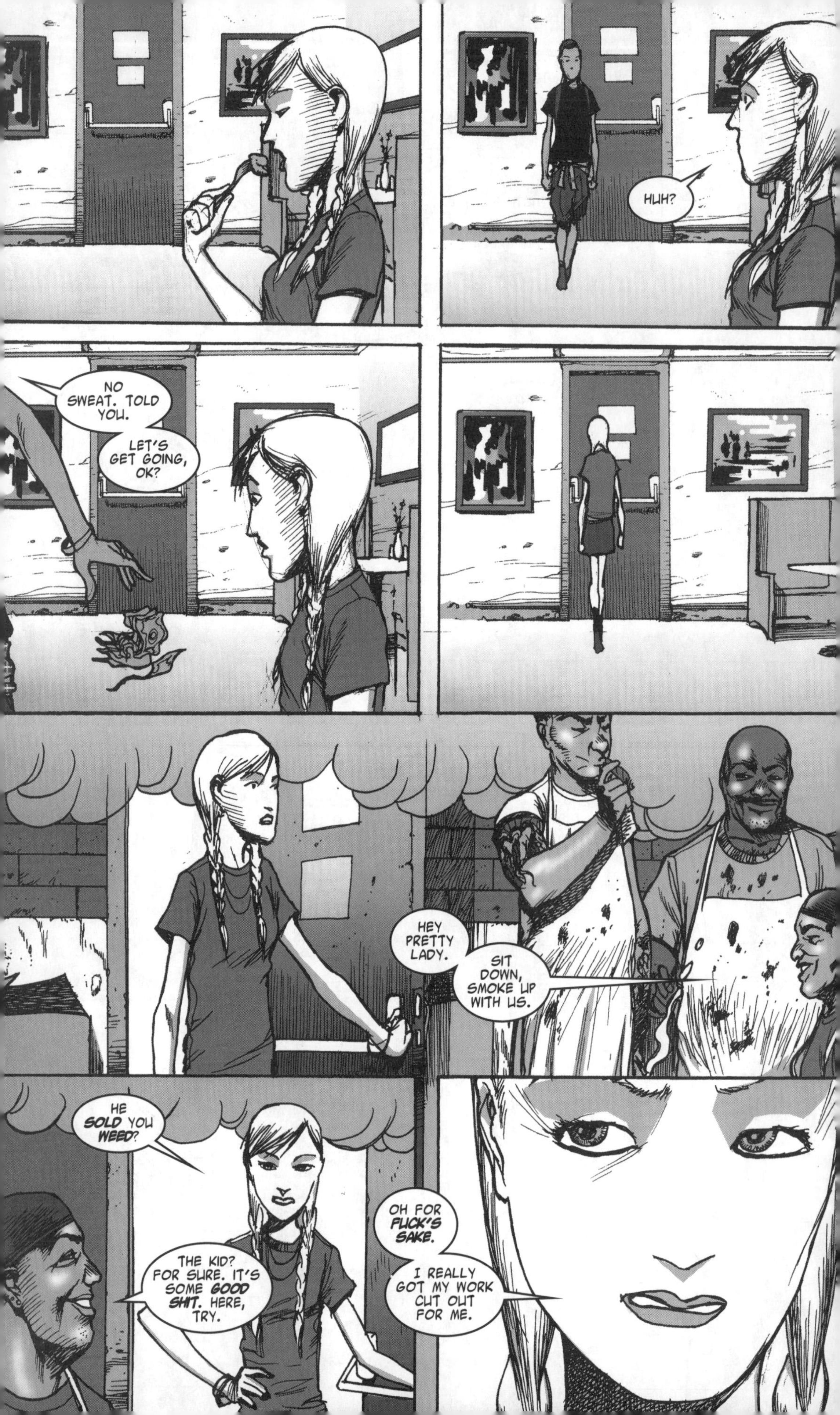
HUH?
NO SWEAT. TOLD YOU.
LET'S GET GOING, OK?
HEY PRETTY LADY.
SIT DOWN, SMOKE UP WITH US.
HE **SOLD** YOU **WEED**?
THE KID? FOR SURE. IT'S SOME **GOOD SHIT**. HERE, TRY.
OH FOR **FUCK'S SAKE.**
I REALLY GOT MY WORK CUT OUT FOR ME.

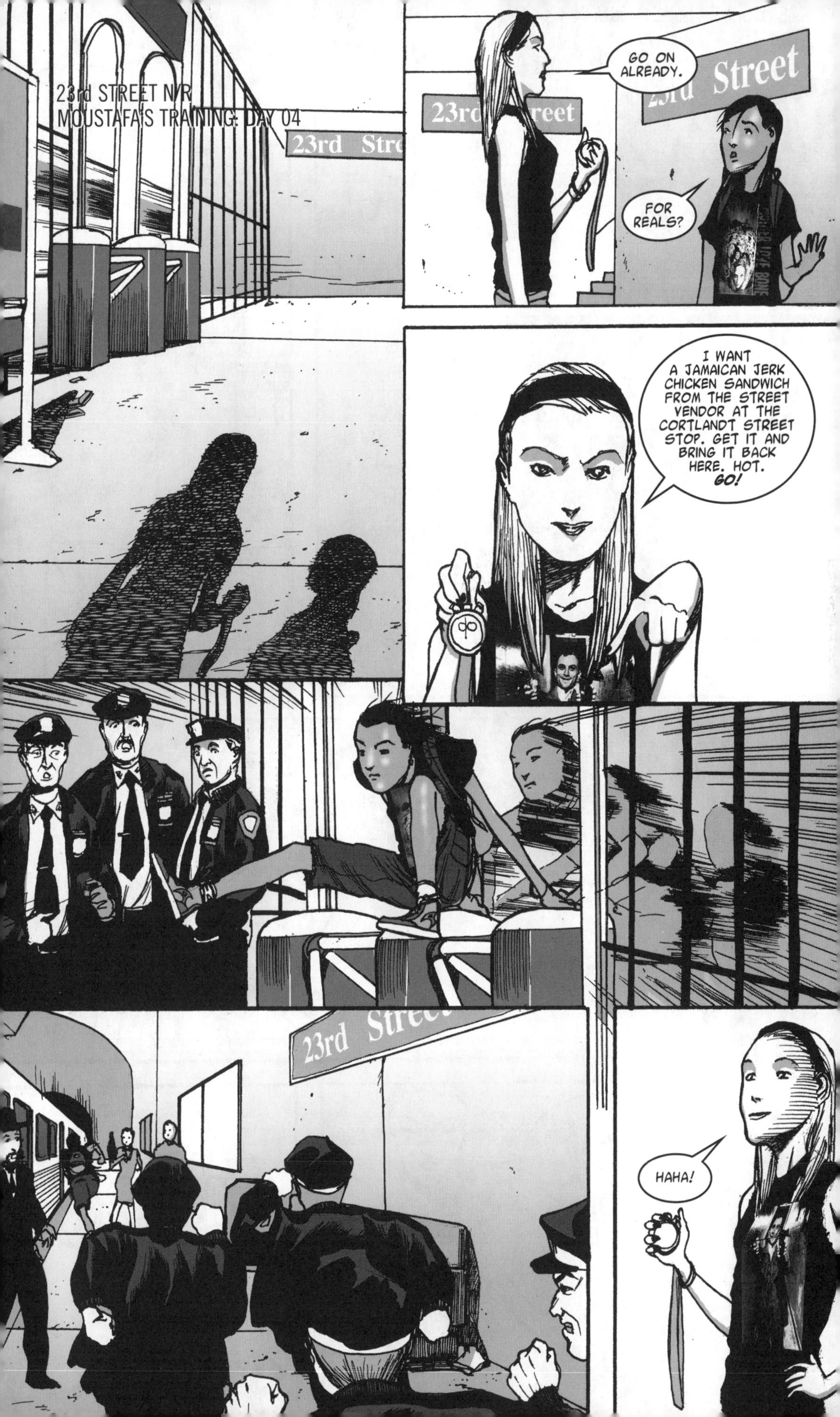
23rd STREET N/R
MOUSTAFA'S TRAINING: DAY 04
23rd Street
GO ON ALREADY.
23rd Street
FOR REALS?
I WANT A JAMAICAN JERK CHICKEN SANDWICH FROM THE STREET VENDOR AT THE CORTLANDT STREET STOP. GET IT AND BRING IT BACK HERE. HOT. GO!
23rd Street
HAHA!

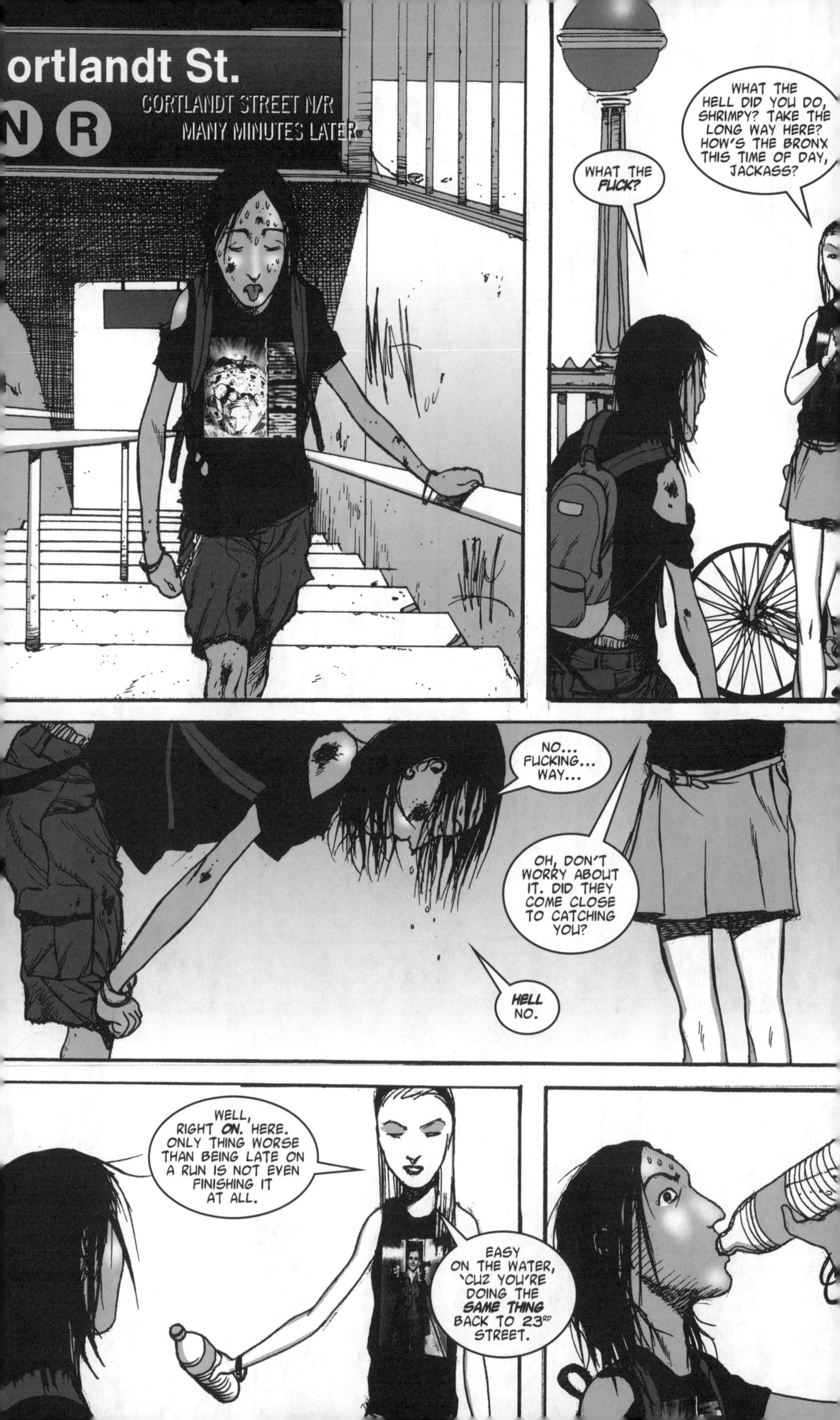
ortlandt St.
N R
CORTLANDT STREET N/R
MANY MINUTES LATER
WHAT THE FUCK?
WHAT THE HELL DID YOU DO, SHRIMPY? TAKE THE LONG WAY HERE? HOW'S THE BRONX THIS TIME OF DAY, JACKASS?
NO... FUCKING... WAY...
OH, DON'T WORRY ABOUT IT. DID THEY COME CLOSE TO CATCHING YOU?
HELL NO.
WELL, RIGHT ON. HERE. ONLY THING WORSE THAN BEING LATE ON A RUN IS NOT EVEN FINISHING IT AT ALL.
EASY ON THE WATER, 'CUZ YOU'RE DOING THE SAME THING BACK TO 23RD STREET.

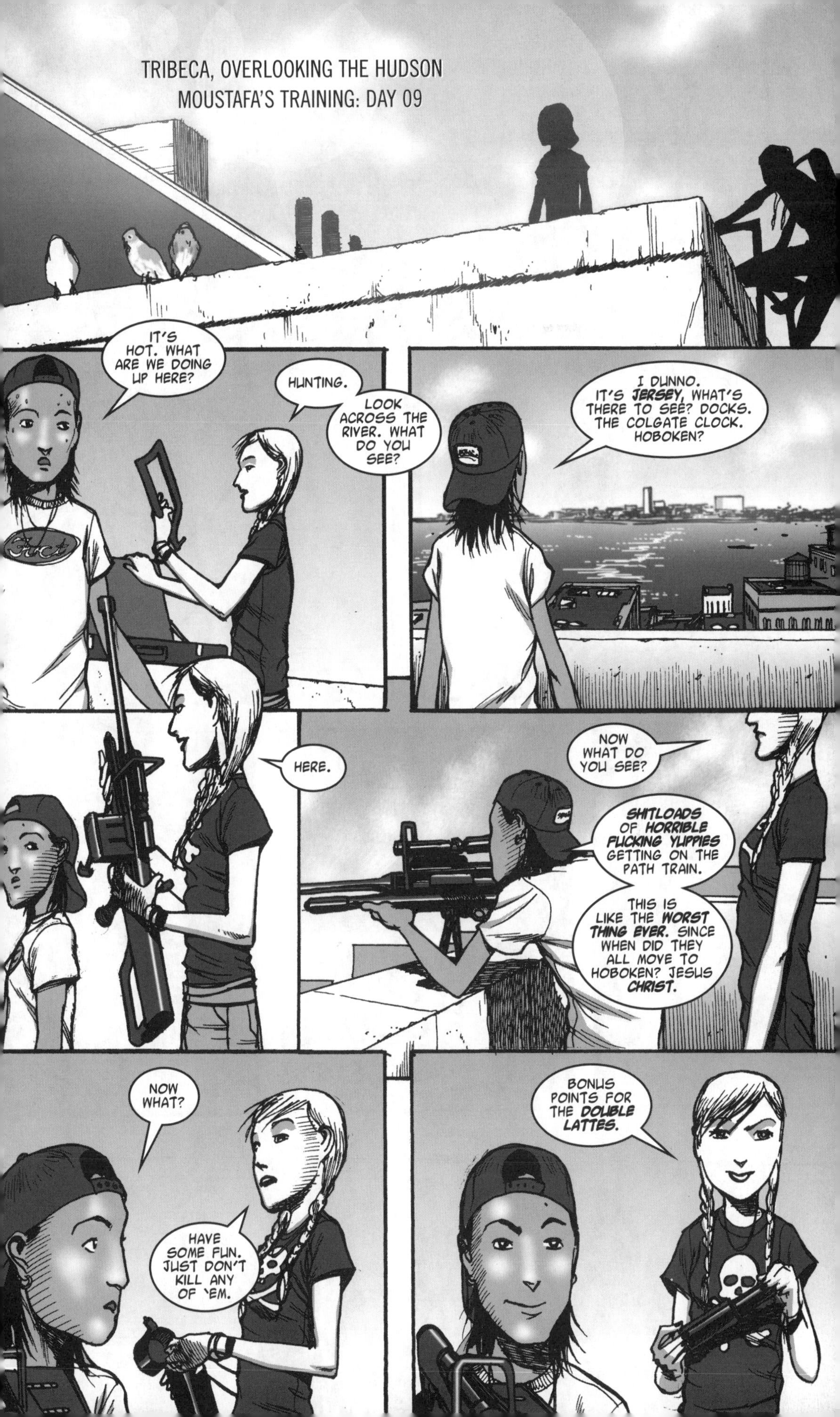
TRIBECA, OVERLOOKING THE HUDSON
MOUSTAFA'S TRAINING: DAY 09
IT'S HOT. WHAT ARE WE DOING UP HERE?
HUNTING.
LOOK ACROSS THE RIVER. WHAT DO YOU SEE?
I DUNNO. IT'S JERSEY, WHAT'S THERE TO SEE? DOCKS. THE COLGATE CLOCK. HOBOKEN?
HERE.
NOW WHAT DO YOU SEE?
SHITLOADS OF HORRIBLE FUCKING YUPPIES GETTING ON THE PATH TRAIN.
THIS IS LIKE THE WORST THING EVER. SINCE WHEN DID THEY ALL MOVE TO HOBOKEN? JESUS CHRIST.
NOW WHAT?
HAVE SOME FUN. JUST DON'T KILL ANY OF 'EM.
BONUS POINTS FOR THE DOUBLE LATTES.

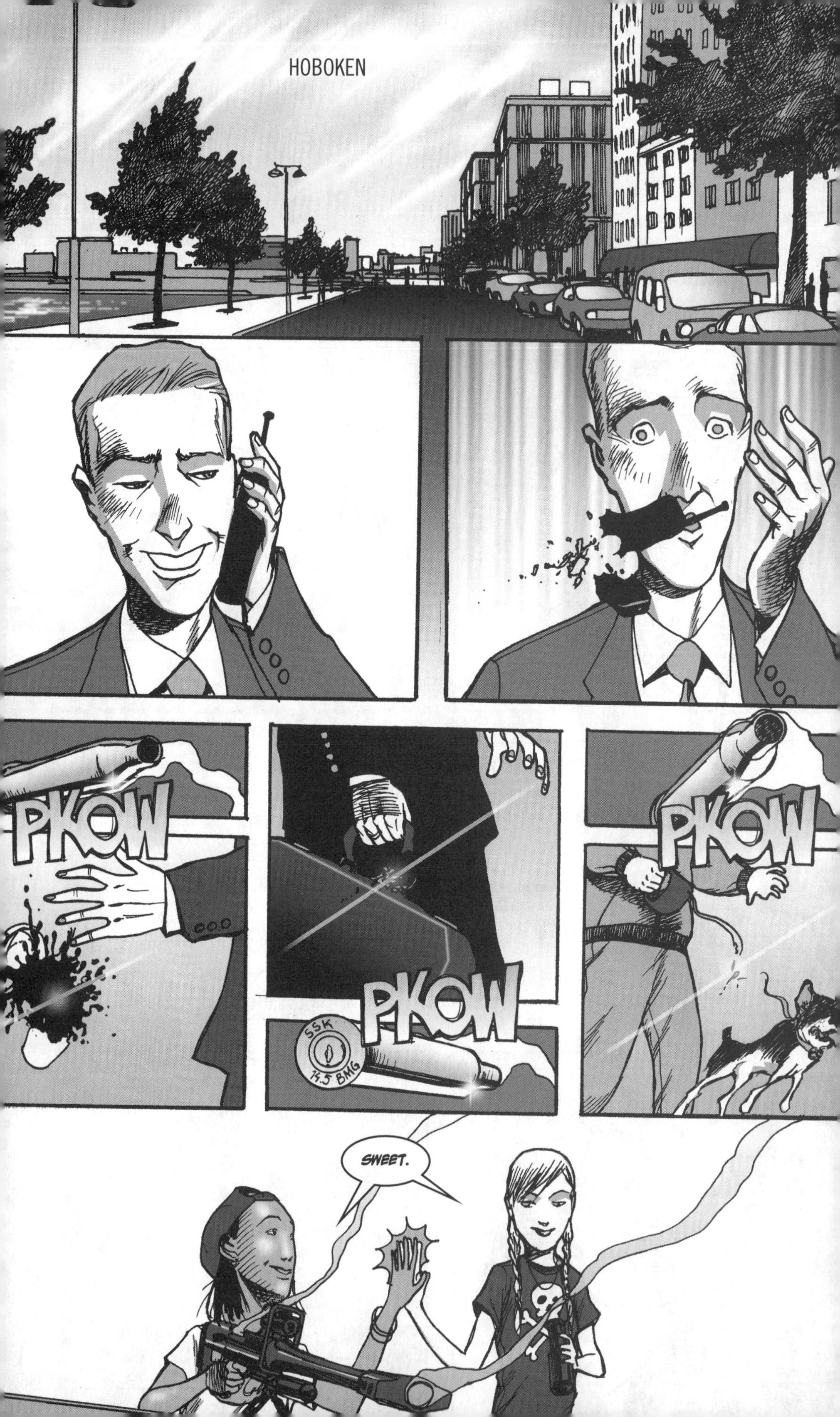
HOBOKEN
PKOW
PKOW
SSK
14.5 BMG
PKOW
SWEET.

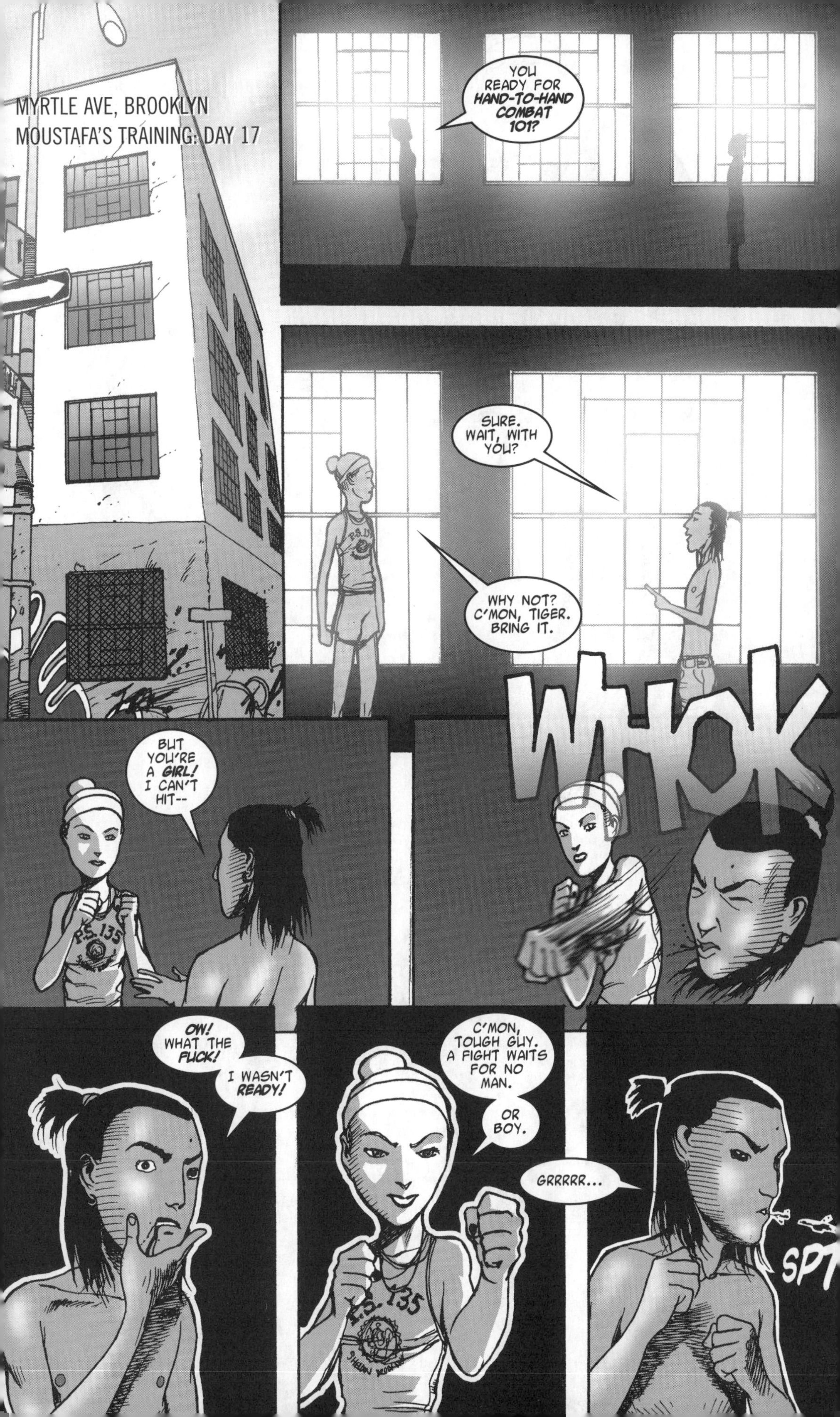
MYRTLE AVE, BROOKLYN
MOUSTAFA'S TRAINING: DAY 17
YOU READY FOR HAND-TO-HAND COMBAT 101?
SURE. WAIT, WITH YOU?
WHY NOT? C'MON, TIGER. BRING IT.
BUT YOU'RE A GIRL! I CAN'T HIT--
WHOK
OW! WHAT THE FUCK!
I WASN'T READY!
C'MON, TOUGH GUY. A FIGHT WAITS FOR NO MAN.
OR BOY.
GRRRRR...
SPT

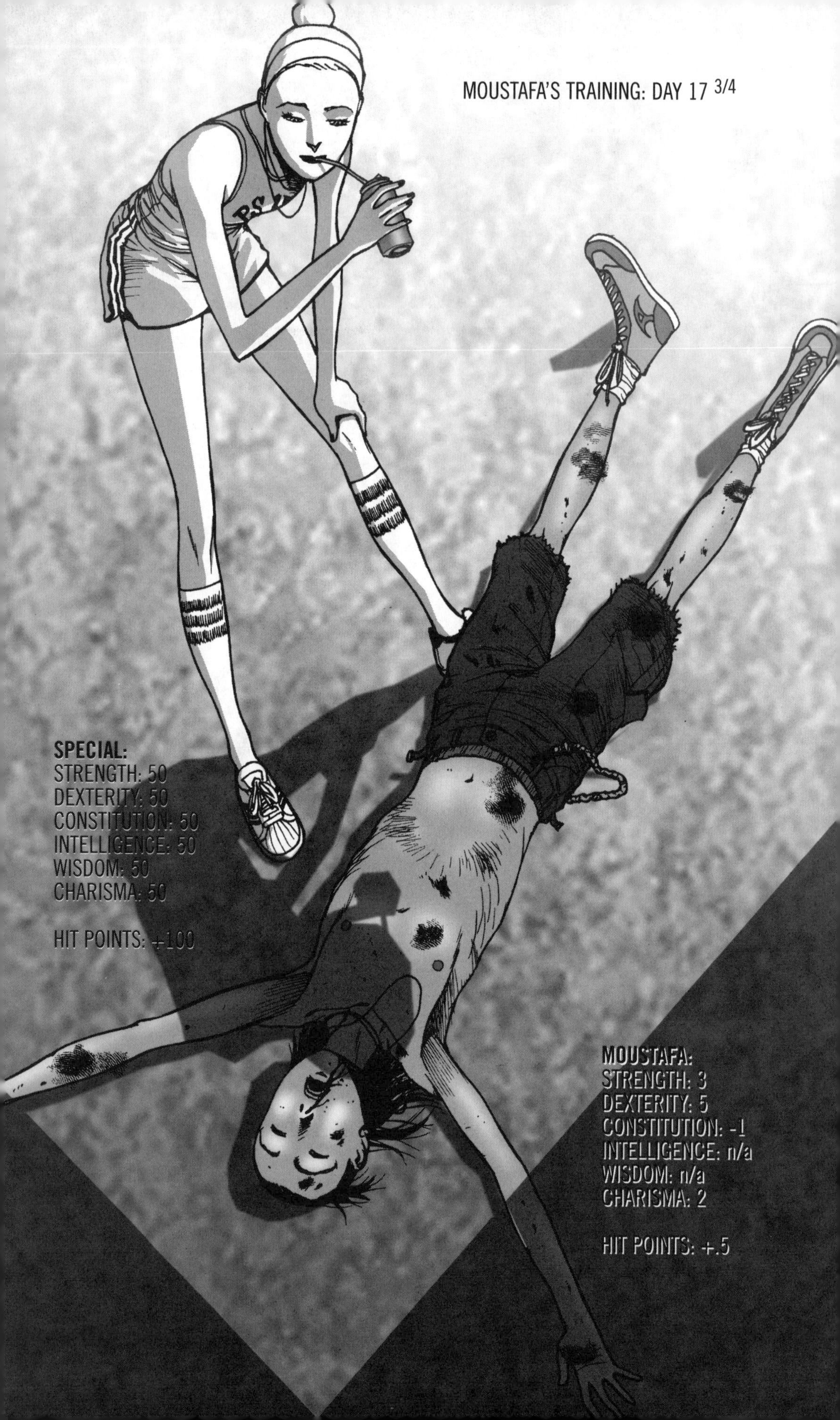
MOUSTAFA'S TRAINING: DAY 17 3/4
SPECIAL:
STRENGTH: 50
DEXTERITY: 50
CONSTITUTION: 50
INTELLIGENCE: 50
WISDOM: 50
CHARISMA: 50
HIT POINTS: +100
MOUSTAFA:
STRENGTH: 3
DEXTERITY: 5
CONSTITUTION: -1
INTELLIGENCE: n/a
WISDOM: n/a
CHARISMA: 2
HIT POINTS: +.5

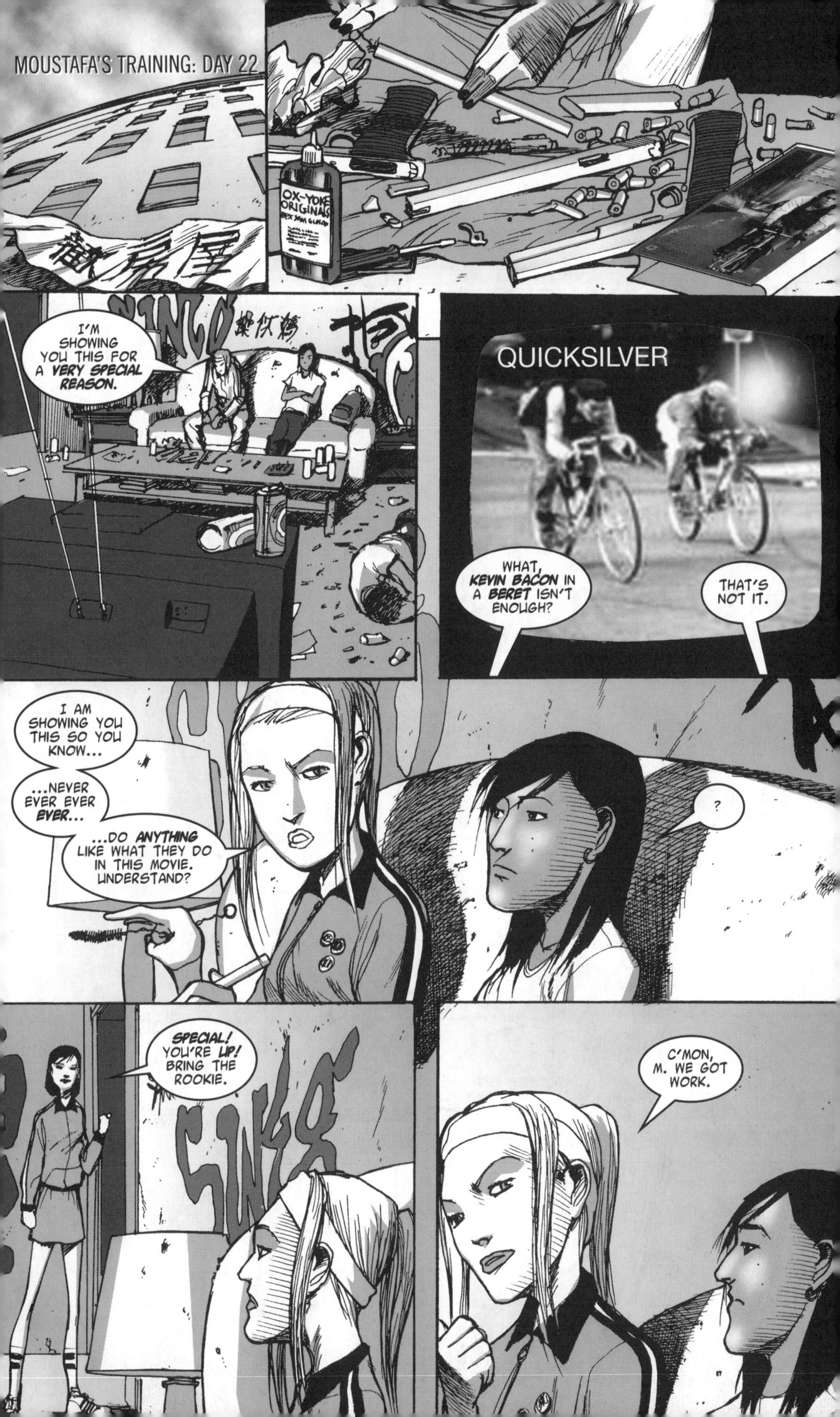
MOUSTAFA'S TRAINING: DAY 22
OX-YOKE ORIGINALS
I'M SHOWING YOU THIS FOR A VERY SPECIAL REASON.
QUICKSILVER
WHAT, KEVIN BACON IN A BERET ISN'T ENOUGH?
THAT'S NOT IT.
I AM SHOWING YOU THIS SO YOU KNOW...
...NEVER EVER EVER EVER...
...DO ANYTHING LIKE WHAT THEY DO IN THIS MOVIE. UNDERSTAND?
?
SPECIAL! YOU'RE UP! BRING THE ROOKIE.
C'MON, M. WE GOT WORK.

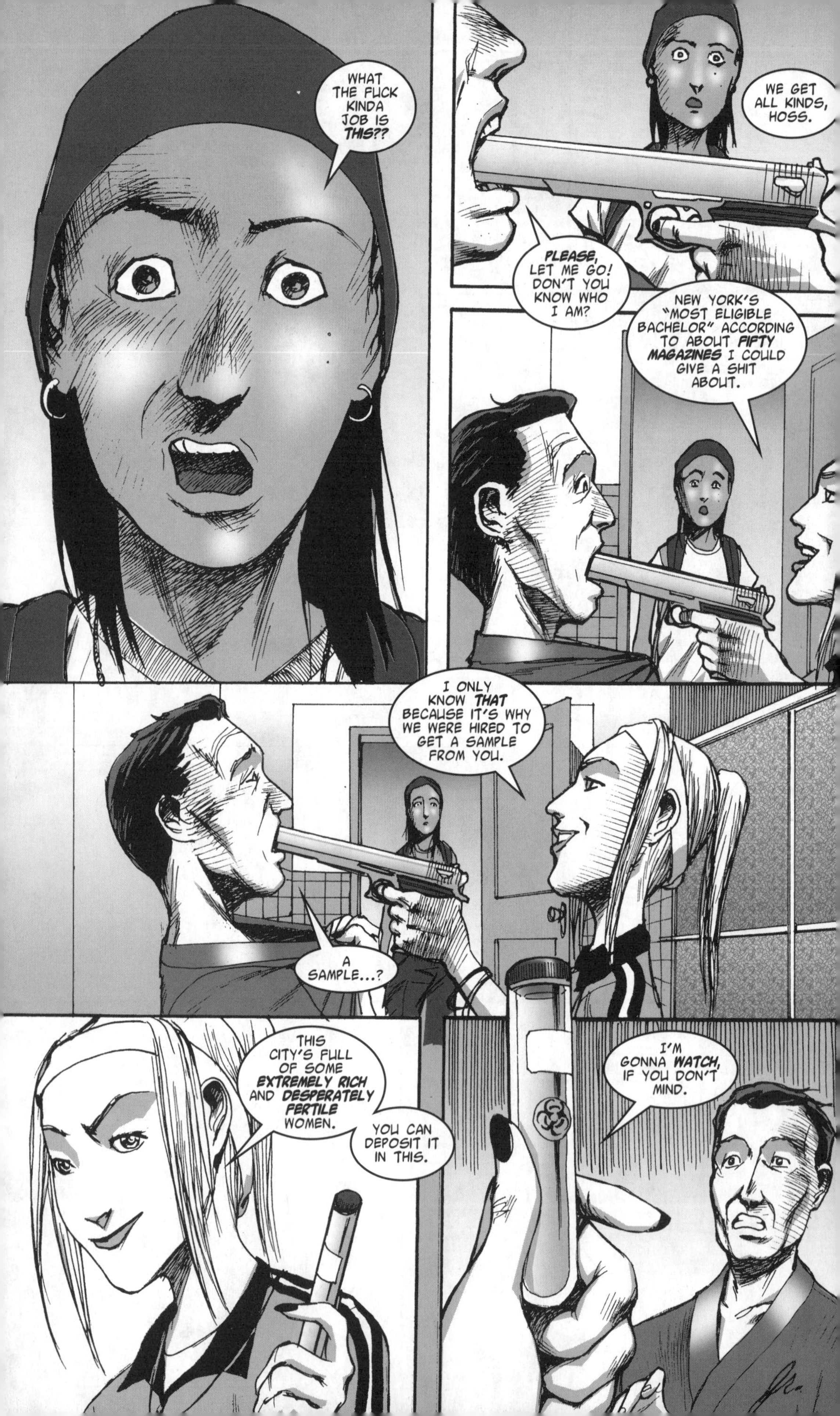

WHAT THE FUCK KINDA JOB IS THIS??
WE GET ALL KINDS, HOSS.
PLEASE, LET ME GO! DON'T YOU KNOW WHO I AM?
NEW YORK'S "MOST ELIGIBLE BACHELOR" ACCORDING TO ABOUT FIFTY MAGAZINES I COULD GIVE A SHIT ABOUT.
I ONLY KNOW THAT BECAUSE IT'S WHY WE WERE HIRED TO GET A SAMPLE FROM YOU.
A SAMPLE...?
THIS CITY'S FULL OF SOME EXTREMELY RICH AND DESPERATELY FERTILE WOMEN.
YOU CAN DEPOSIT IT IN THIS.
I'M GONNA WATCH, IF YOU DON'T MIND.

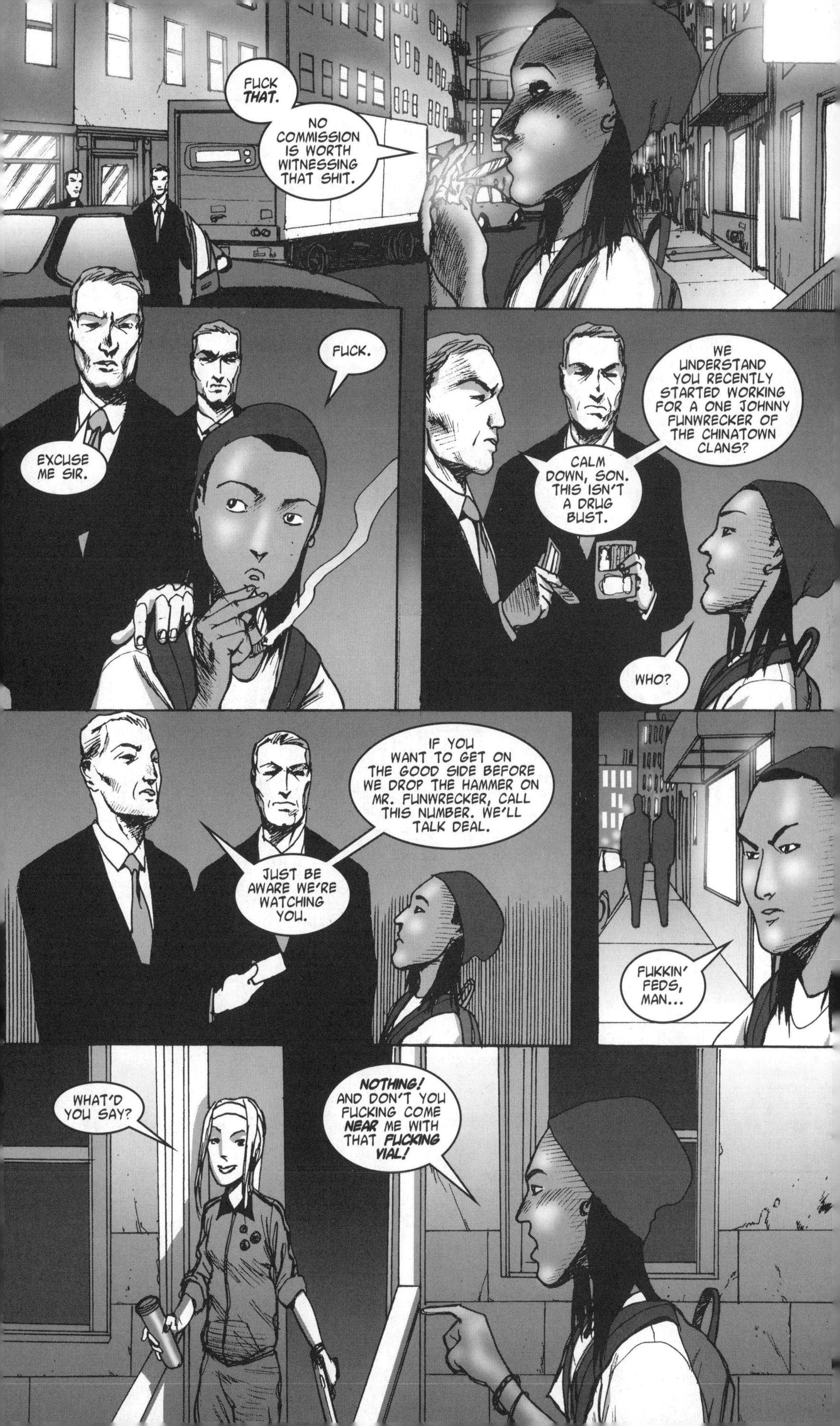
FUCK THAT.
NO COMMISSION IS WORTH WITNESSING THAT SHIT.
FUCK.
EXCUSE ME SIR.
WE UNDERSTAND YOU RECENTLY STARTED WORKING FOR A ONE JOHNNY FUNWRECKER OF THE CHINATOWN CLANS?
CALM DOWN, SON. THIS ISN'T A DRUG BUST.
WHO?
IF YOU WANT TO GET ON THE GOOD SIDE BEFORE WE DROP THE HAMMER ON MR. FUNWRECKER, CALL THIS NUMBER. WE'LL TALK DEAL.
JUST BE AWARE WE'RE WATCHING YOU.
FUKKIN' FEDS, MAN...
WHAT'D YOU SAY?
NOTHING! AND DON'T YOU FUCKING COME NEAR ME WITH THAT FUCKING VIAL!

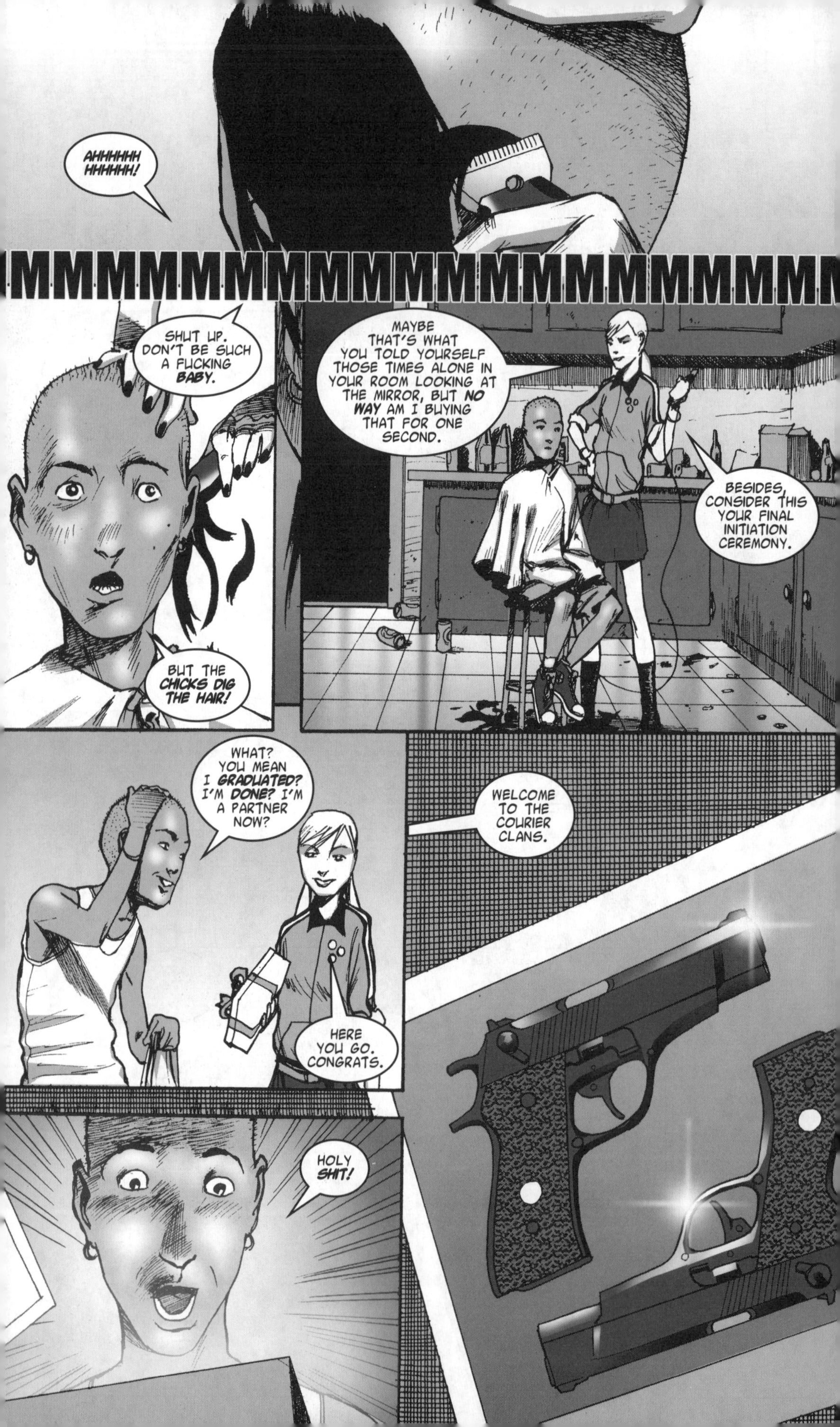
AHHHHHH HHHHHH!
MMMMMMMMMMMMMMMMMMMMMMM
SHUT UP. DON'T BE SUCH A FUCKING BABY.
BUT THE CHICKS DIG THE HAIR!
MAYBE THAT'S WHAT YOU TOLD YOURSELF THOSE TIMES ALONE IN YOUR ROOM LOOKING AT THE MIRROR, BUT NO WAY AM I BUYING THAT FOR ONE SECOND.
BESIDES, CONSIDER THIS YOUR FINAL INITIATION CEREMONY.
WHAT? YOU MEAN I GRADUATED? I'M DONE? I'M A PARTNER NOW?
HERE YOU GO. CONGRATS.
WELCOME TO THE COURIER CLANS.
HOLY SHIT!

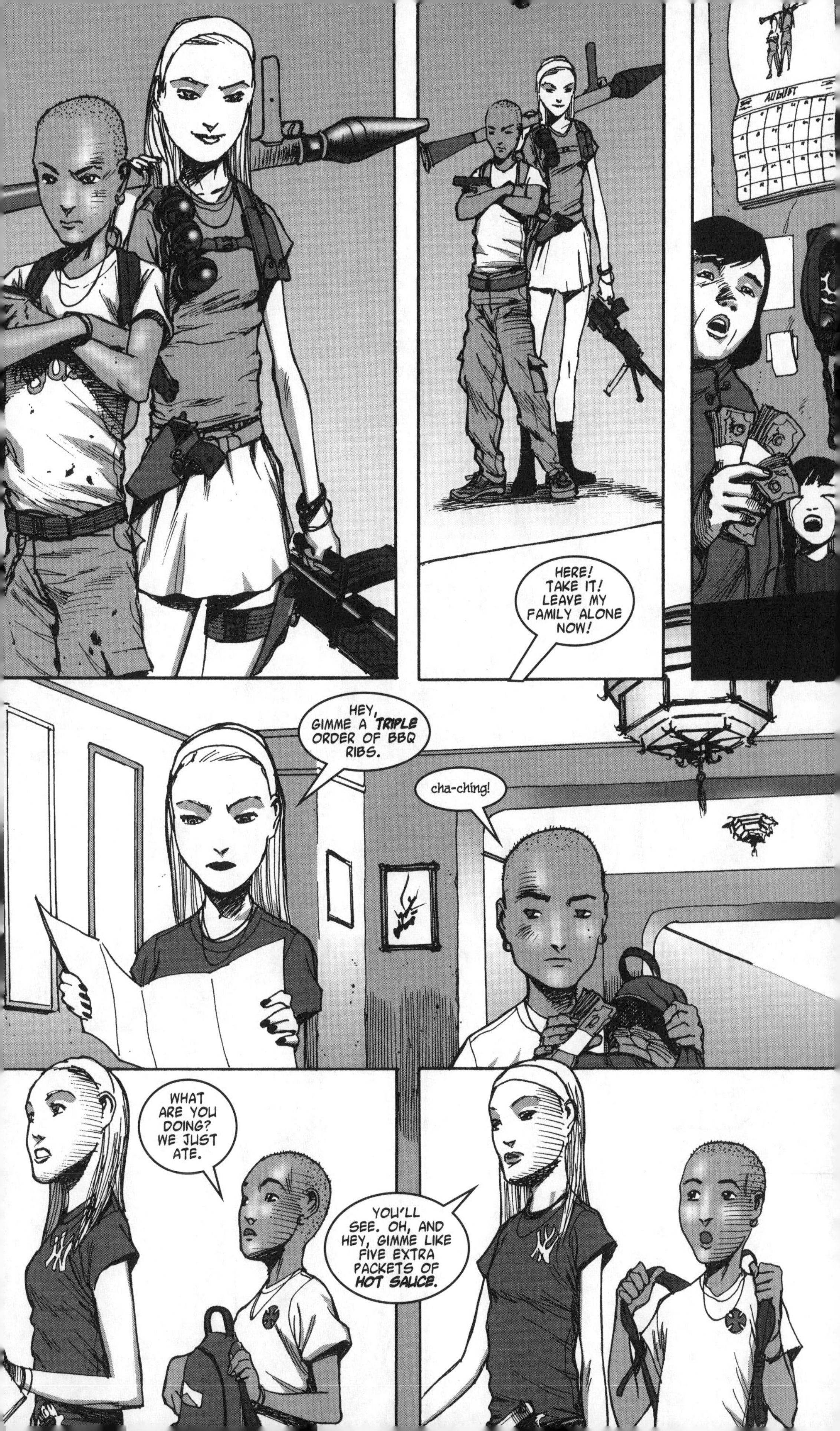
AUGUST
HERE! TAKE IT! LEAVE MY FAMILY ALONE NOW!
HEY, GIMME A TRIPLE ORDER OF BBQ RIBS.
cha-ching!
WHAT ARE YOU DOING? WE JUST ATE.
YOU'LL SEE. OH, AND HEY, GIMME LIKE FIVE EXTRA PACKETS OF HOT SAUCE.

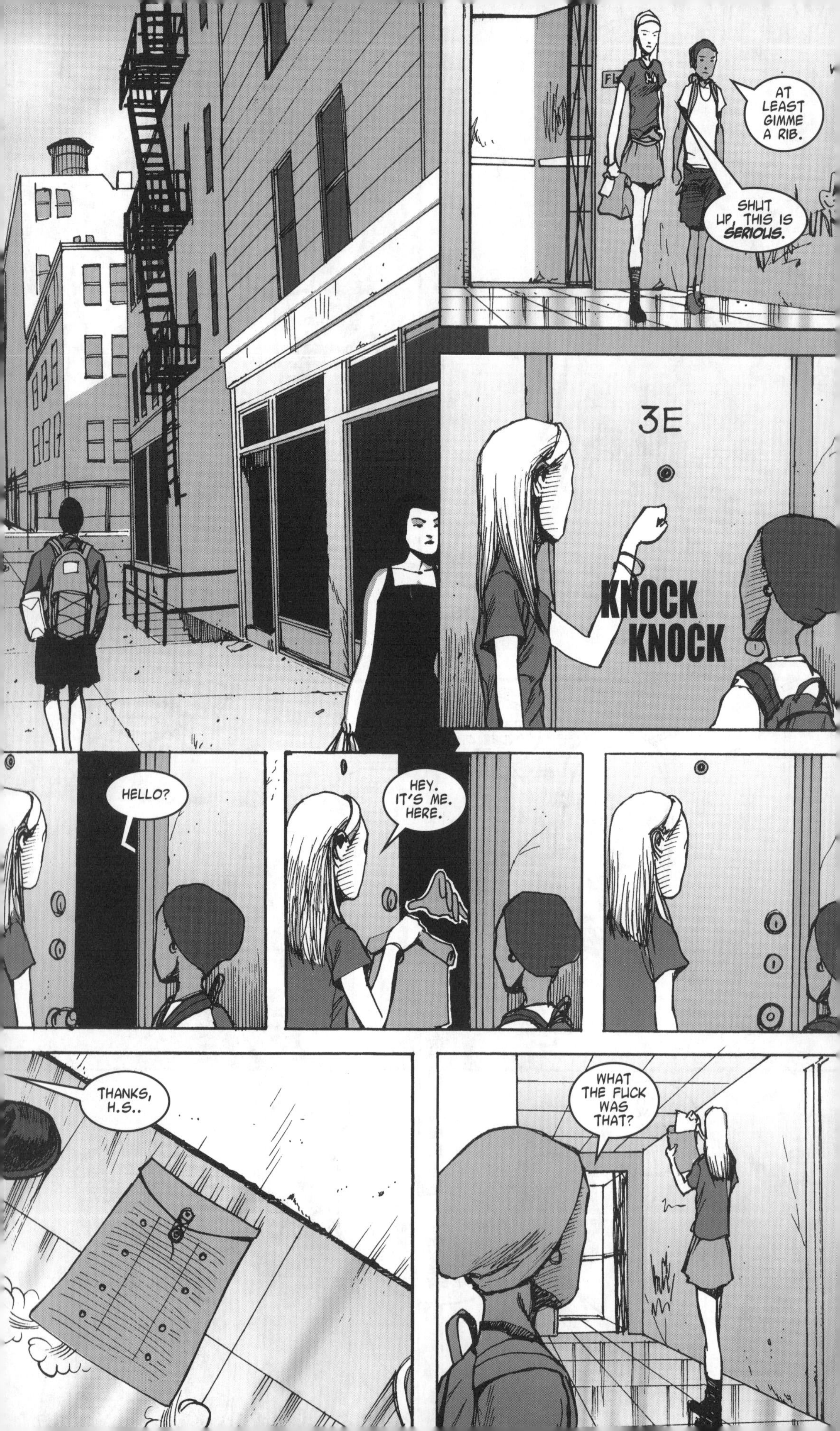
AT LEAST GIMME A RIB.
SHUT UP, THIS IS SERIOUS.
3E
KNOCK KNOCK
HELLO?
HEY. IT'S ME. HERE.
THANKS, H.S..
WHAT THE FUCK WAS THAT?

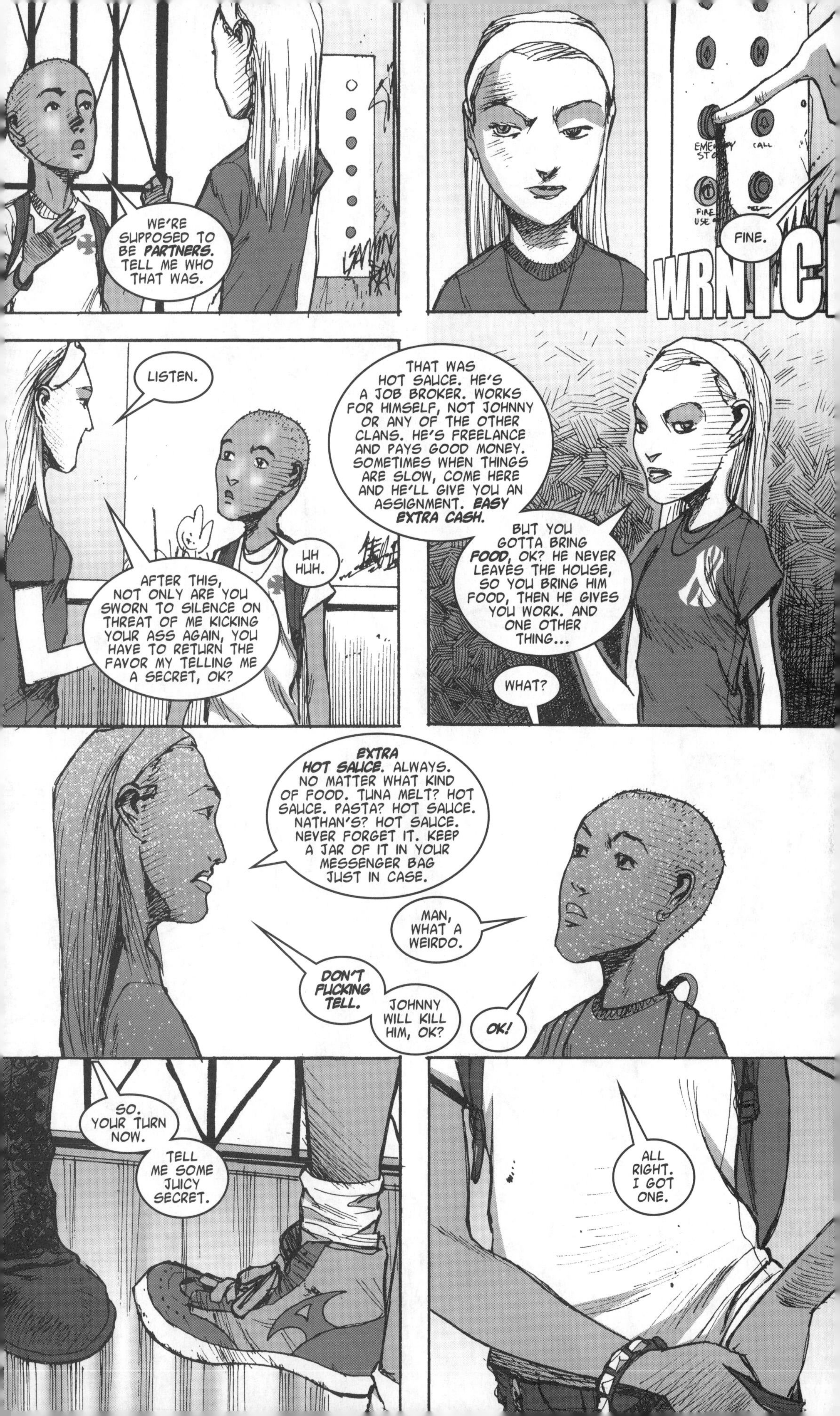
WE'RE SUPPOSED TO BE PARTNERS. TELL ME WHO THAT WAS.
EMERGENCY STOP
CALL
FIRE USE
FINE.
WRNTCH
LISTEN.
AFTER THIS, NOT ONLY ARE YOU SWORN TO SILENCE ON THREAT OF ME KICKING YOUR ASS AGAIN, YOU HAVE TO RETURN THE FAVOR MY TELLING ME A SECRET, OK?
UH HUH.
THAT WAS HOT SAUCE. HE'S A JOB BROKER. WORKS FOR HIMSELF, NOT JOHNNY OR ANY OF THE OTHER CLANS. HE'S FREELANCE AND PAYS GOOD MONEY. SOMETIMES WHEN THINGS ARE SLOW, COME HERE AND HE'LL GIVE YOU AN ASSIGNMENT. EASY EXTRA CASH.
BUT YOU GOTTA BRING FOOD, OK? HE NEVER LEAVES THE HOUSE, SO YOU BRING HIM FOOD, THEN HE GIVES YOU WORK. AND ONE OTHER THING...
WHAT?
EXTRA HOT SAUCE. ALWAYS. NO MATTER WHAT KIND OF FOOD. TUNA MELT? HOT SAUCE. PASTA? HOT SAUCE. NATHAN'S? HOT SAUCE. NEVER FORGET IT. KEEP A JAR OF IT IN YOUR MESSENGER BAG JUST IN CASE.
MAN, WHAT A WEIRDO.
DON'T FUCKING TELL.
JOHNNY WILL KILL HIM, OK?
OK!
SO. YOUR TURN NOW.
TELL ME SOME JUICY SECRET.
ALL RIGHT. I GOT ONE.

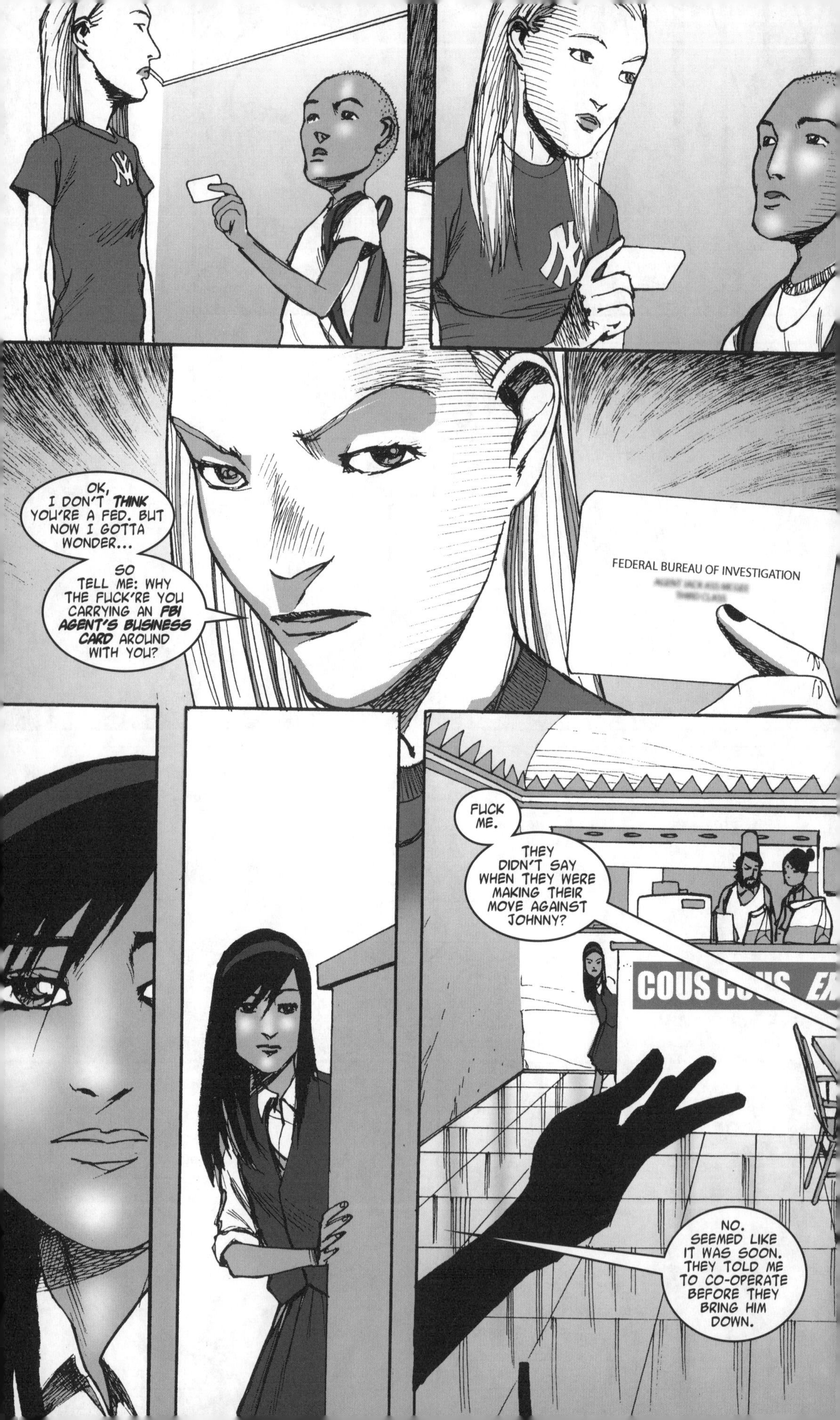

OK, I DON'T **THINK** YOU'RE A FED. BUT NOW I GOTTA WONDER...
SO TELL ME: WHY THE FUCK'RE YOU CARRYING AN **FBI AGENT'S BUSINESS CARD** AROUND WITH YOU?
FEDERAL BUREAU OF INVESTIGATION
FUCK ME.
THEY DIDN'T SAY WHEN THEY WERE MAKING THEIR MOVE AGAINST JOHNNY?
COUS
NO. SEEMED LIKE IT WAS SOON. THEY TOLD ME TO CO-OPERATE BEFORE THEY BRING HIM DOWN.

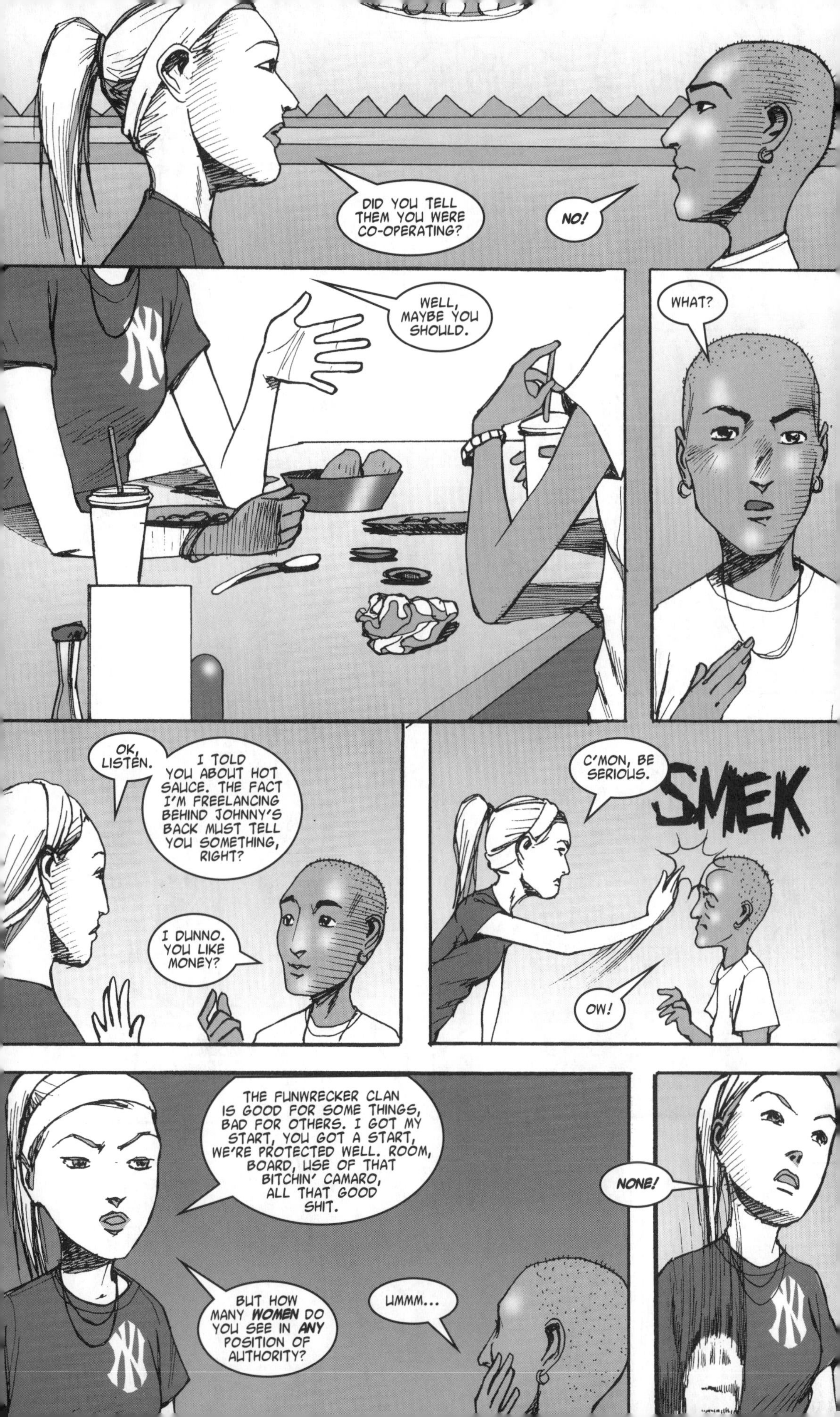
DID YOU TELL THEM YOU WERE CO-OPERATING?
NO!
WELL, MAYBE YOU SHOULD.
WHAT?
OK, LISTEN.
I TOLD YOU ABOUT HOT SAUCE. THE FACT I'M FREELANCING BEHIND JOHNNY'S BACK MUST TELL YOU SOMETHING, RIGHT?
I DUNNO. YOU LIKE MONEY?
C'MON, BE SERIOUS.
SMEK
OW!
THE FUNWRECKER CLAN IS GOOD FOR SOME THINGS, BAD FOR OTHERS. I GOT MY START, YOU GOT A START, WE'RE PROTECTED WELL. ROOM, BOARD, USE OF THAT BITCHIN' CAMARO, ALL THAT GOOD SHIT.
BUT HOW MANY **WOMEN** DO YOU SEE IN **ANY** POSITION OF AUTHORITY?
UMMM...
NONE!

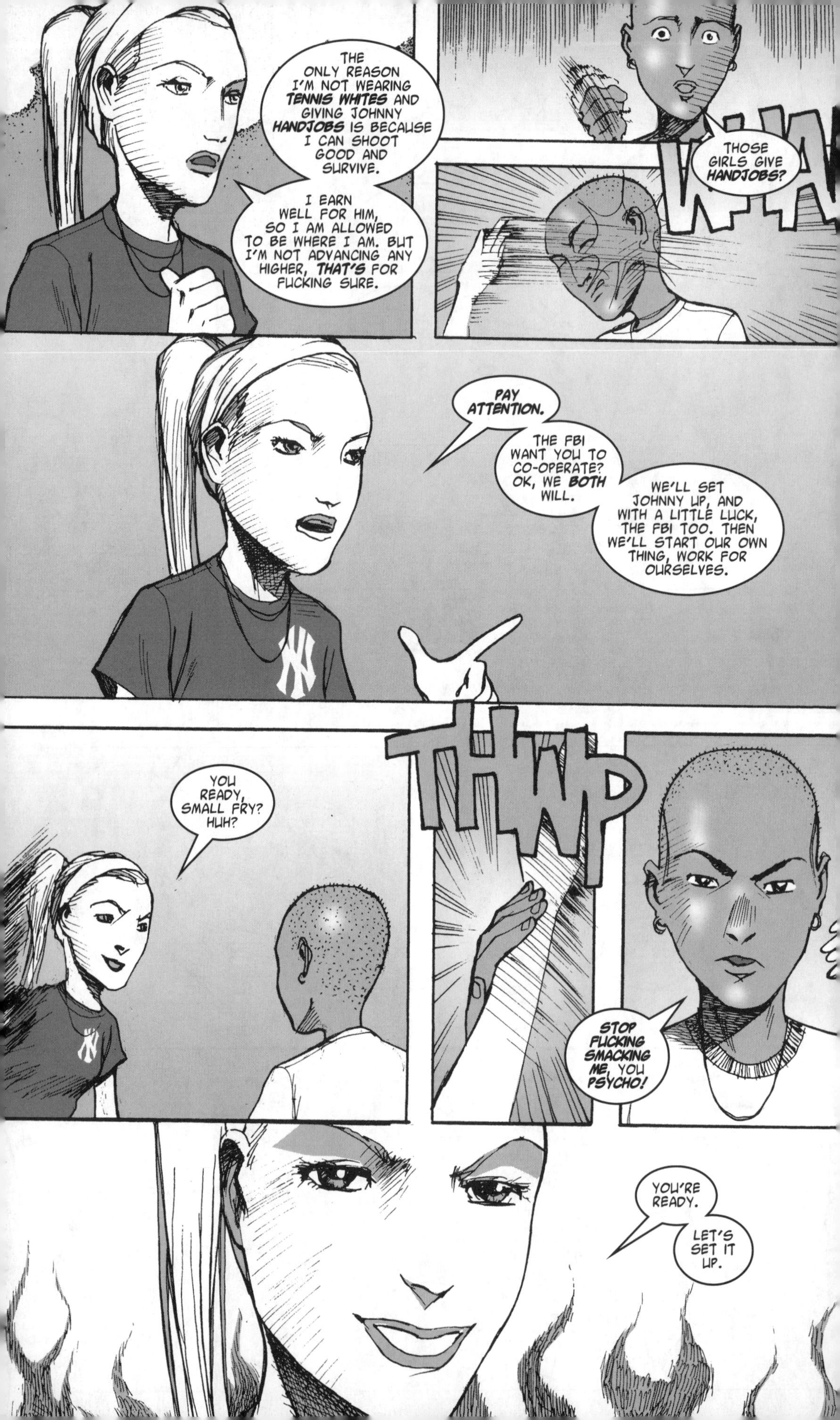
THE ONLY REASON I'M NOT WEARING TENNIS WHITES AND GIVING JOHNNY HANDJOBS IS BECAUSE I CAN SHOOT GOOD AND SURVIVE.
I EARN WELL FOR HIM, SO I AM ALLOWED TO BE WHERE I AM. BUT I'M NOT ADVANCING ANY HIGHER, THAT'S FOR FUCKING SURE.
THOSE GIRLS GIVE HANDJOBS?
PAY ATTENTION.
THE FBI WANT YOU TO CO-OPERATE? OK, WE BOTH WILL.
WE'LL SET JOHNNY UP, AND WITH A LITTLE LUCK, THE FBI TOO. THEN WE'LL START OUR OWN THING, WORK FOR OURSELVES.
YOU READY, SMALL FRY? HUH?
THWP
STOP FUCKING SMACKING ME, YOU PSYCHO!
YOU'RE READY.
LET'S SET IT UP.

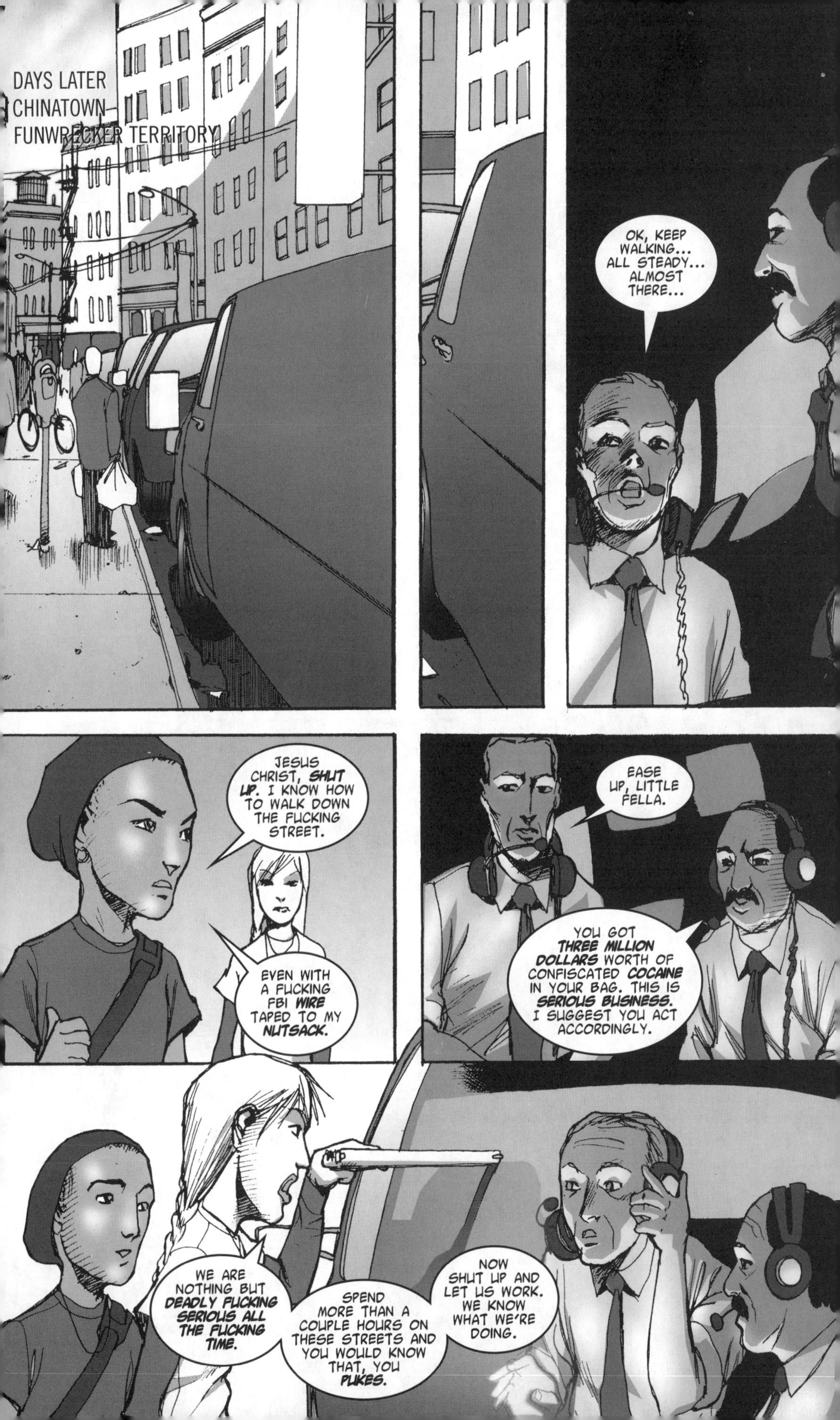
DAYS LATER
CHINATOWN–
FUNWRECKER TERRITORY
OK, KEEP WALKING... ALL STEADY... ALMOST THERE...
JESUS CHRIST, SHUT UP. I KNOW HOW TO WALK DOWN THE FUCKING STREET.
EVEN WITH A FUCKING FBI WIRE TAPED TO MY NUTSACK.
EASE UP, LITTLE FELLA.
YOU GOT THREE MILLION DOLLARS WORTH OF CONFISCATED COCAINE IN YOUR BAG. THIS IS SERIOUS BUSINESS. I SUGGEST YOU ACT ACCORDINGLY.
WE ARE NOTHING BUT DEADLY FUCKING SERIOUS ALL THE FUCKING TIME.
SPEND MORE THAN A COUPLE HOURS ON THESE STREETS AND YOU WOULD KNOW THAT, YOU PUKES.
NOW SHUT UP AND LET US WORK. WE KNOW WHAT WE'RE DOING.

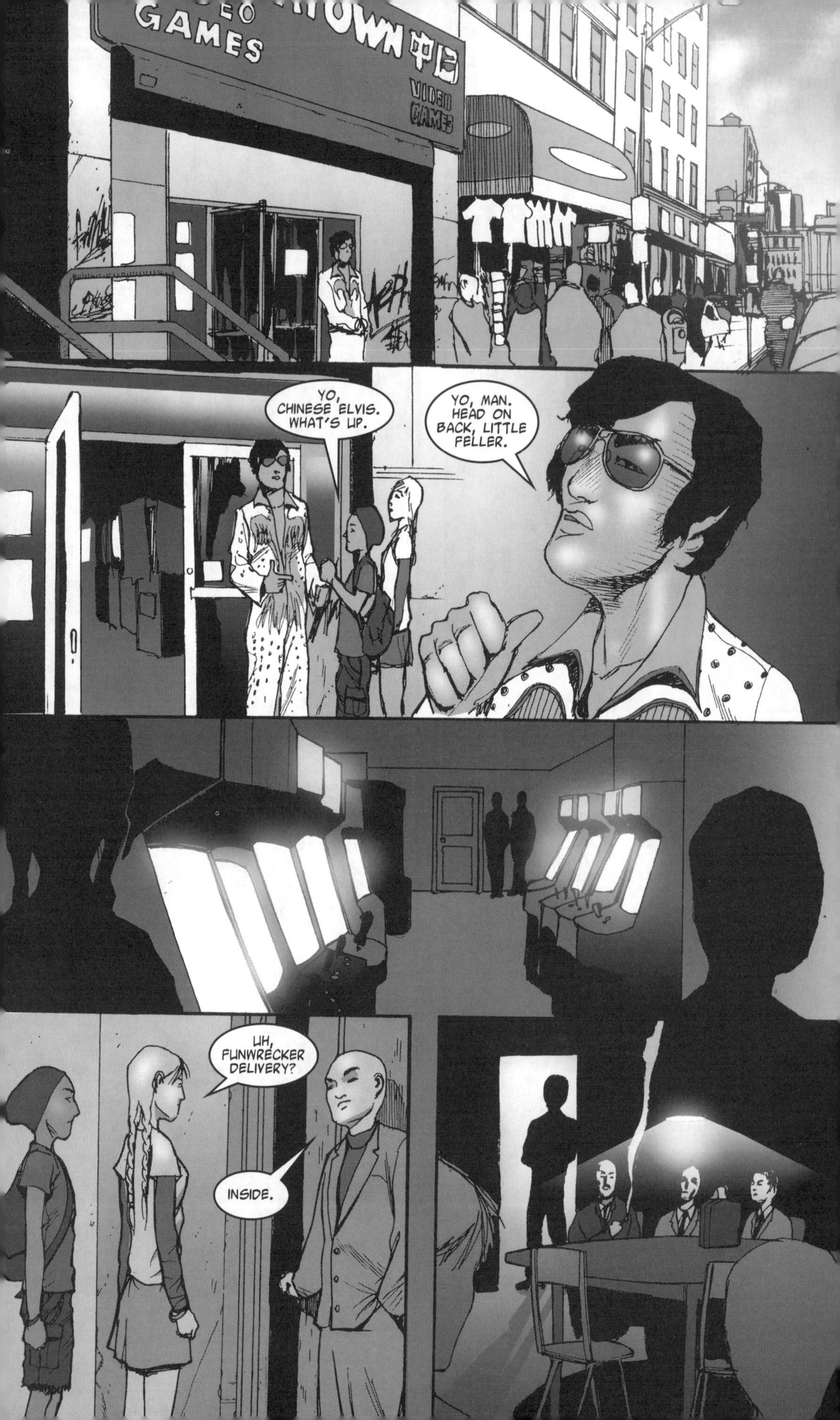
GAMES
VIDEO GAMES
YO, CHINESE ELVIS. WHAT'S UP.
YO, MAN. HEAD ON BACK, LITTLE FELLER.
UH, FUNWRECKER DELIVERY?
INSIDE.

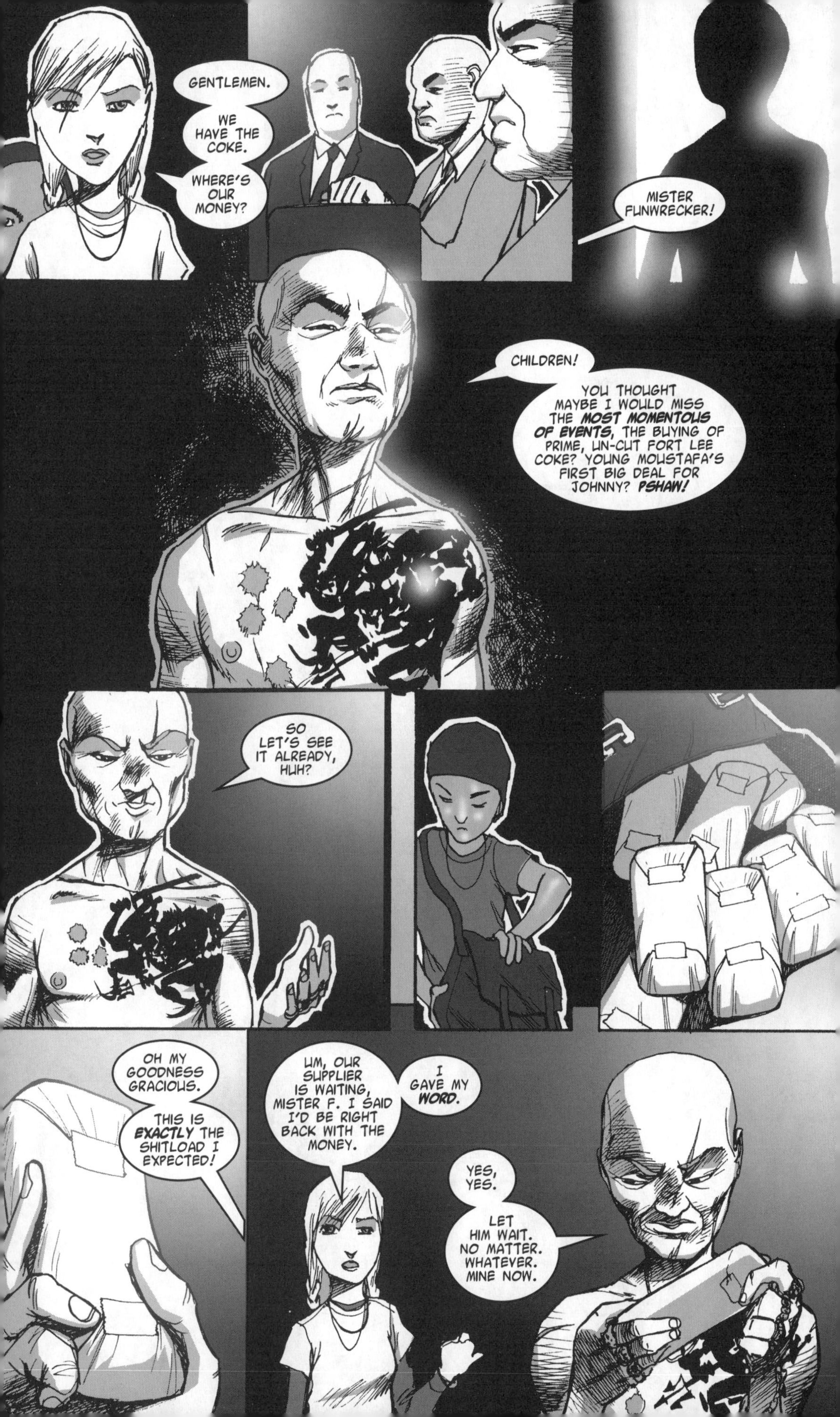
GENTLEMEN.
WE HAVE THE COKE.
WHERE'S OUR MONEY?
MISTER FUNWRECKER!
CHILDREN!
YOU THOUGHT MAYBE I WOULD MISS THE **MOST MOMENTOUS OF EVENTS**, THE BUYING OF PRIME, UN-CUT FORT LEE COKE? YOUNG MOUSTAFA'S FIRST BIG DEAL FOR JOHNNY? **PSHAW!**
SO LET'S SEE IT ALREADY, HUH?
OH MY GOODNESS GRACIOUS.
THIS IS **EXACTLY** THE SHITLOAD I EXPECTED!
UM, OUR SUPPLIER IS WAITING, MISTER F. I SAID I'D BE RIGHT BACK WITH THE MONEY.
I GAVE MY **WORD**.
YES, YES.
LET HIM WAIT. NO MATTER. WHATEVER. MINE NOW.

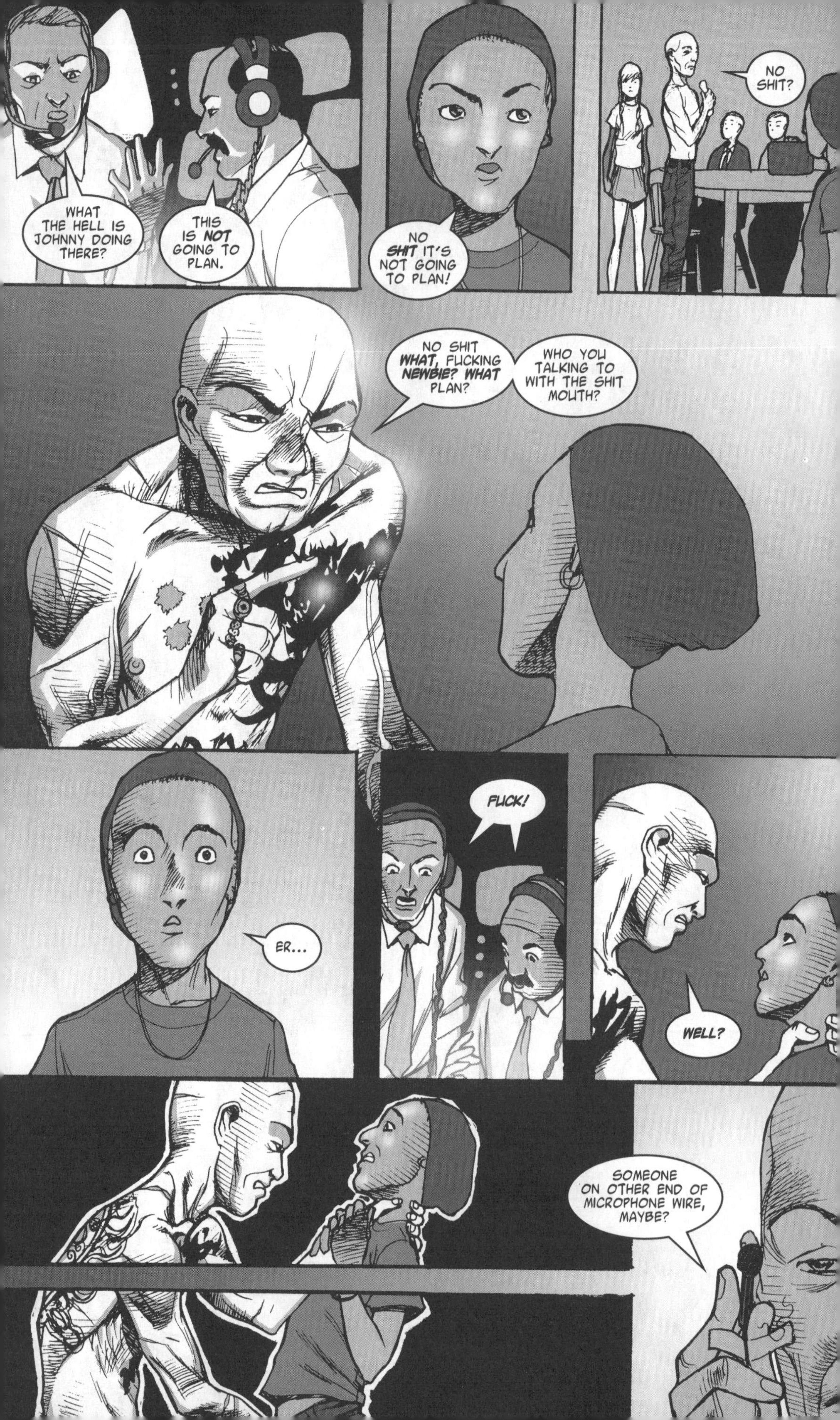
WHAT THE HELL IS JOHNNY DOING THERE?
THIS IS **NOT** GOING TO PLAN.
NO **SHIT** IT'S NOT GOING TO PLAN!
NO SHIT?
NO SHIT **WHAT,** FUCKING **NEWBIE? WHAT** PLAN?
WHO YOU TALKING TO WITH THE SHIT MOUTH?
ER...
FUCK!
WELL?
SOMEONE ON OTHER END OF MICROPHONE WIRE, MAYBE?

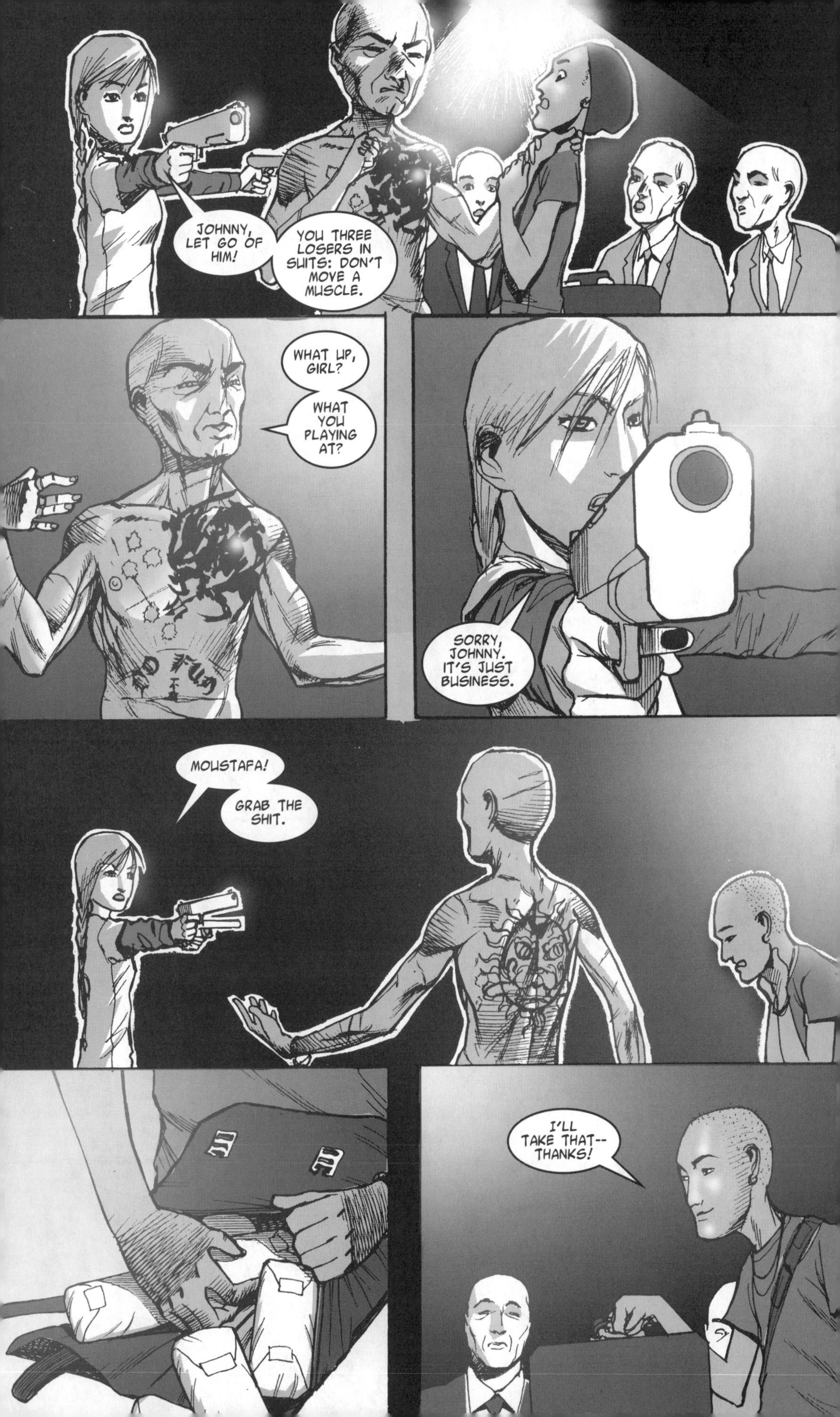
JOHNNY, LET GO OF HIM!
YOU THREE LOSERS IN SUITS: DON'T MOVE A MUSCLE.
WHAT UP, GIRL?
WHAT YOU PLAYING AT?
SORRY, JOHNNY. IT'S JUST BUSINESS.
MOUSTAFA!
GRAB THE SHIT.
I'LL TAKE THAT-- THANKS!

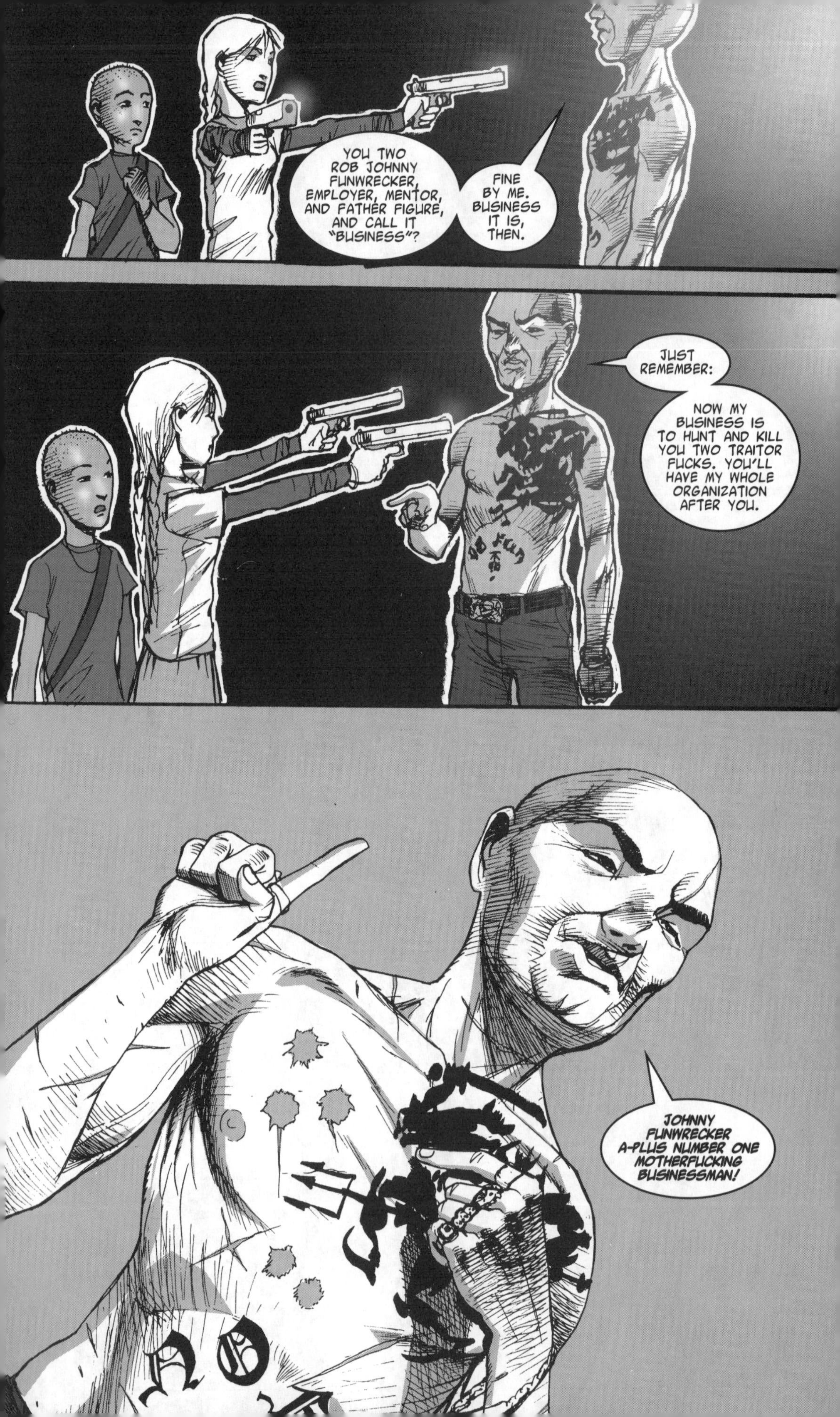
YOU TWO ROB JOHNNY FUNWRECKER, EMPLOYER, MENTOR, AND FATHER FIGURE, AND CALL IT "BUSINESS"?
FINE BY ME. BUSINESS IT IS, THEN.
JUST REMEMBER:
NOW MY BUSINESS IS TO HUNT AND KILL YOU TWO TRAITOR FUCKS. YOU'LL HAVE MY WHOLE ORGANIZATION AFTER YOU.
JOHNNY FUNWRECKER A-PLUS NUMBER ONE MOTHERFUCKING BUSINESSMAN!

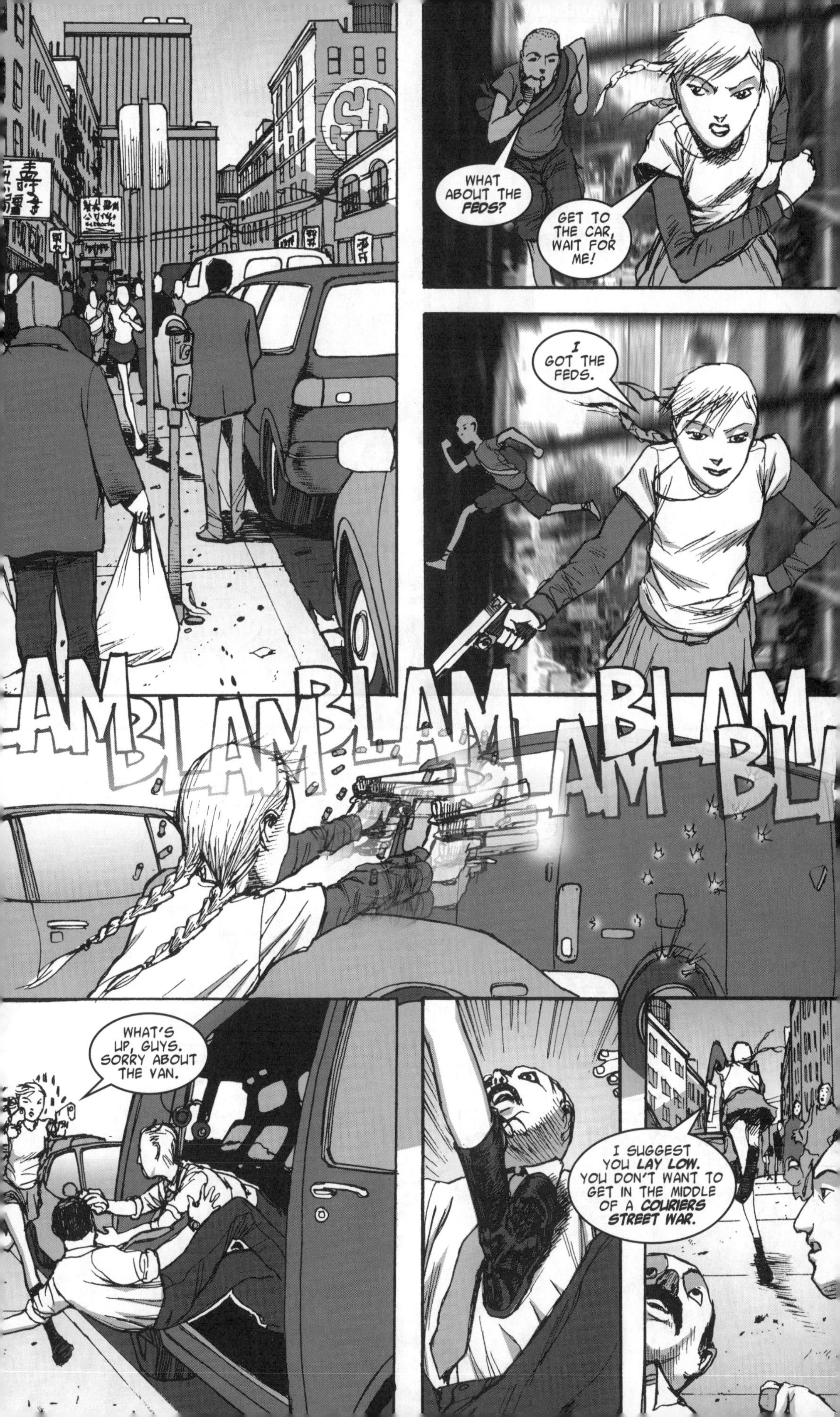
WHAT ABOUT THE FEDS?
GET TO THE CAR, WAIT FOR ME!
I GOT THE FEDS.
BLAM BLAM BLAM BLAM BLAM BLAM BLAM BLAM
WHAT'S UP, GUYS. SORRY ABOUT THE VAN.
I SUGGEST YOU LAY LOW. YOU DON'T WANT TO GET IN THE MIDDLE OF A COURIERS STREET WAR.

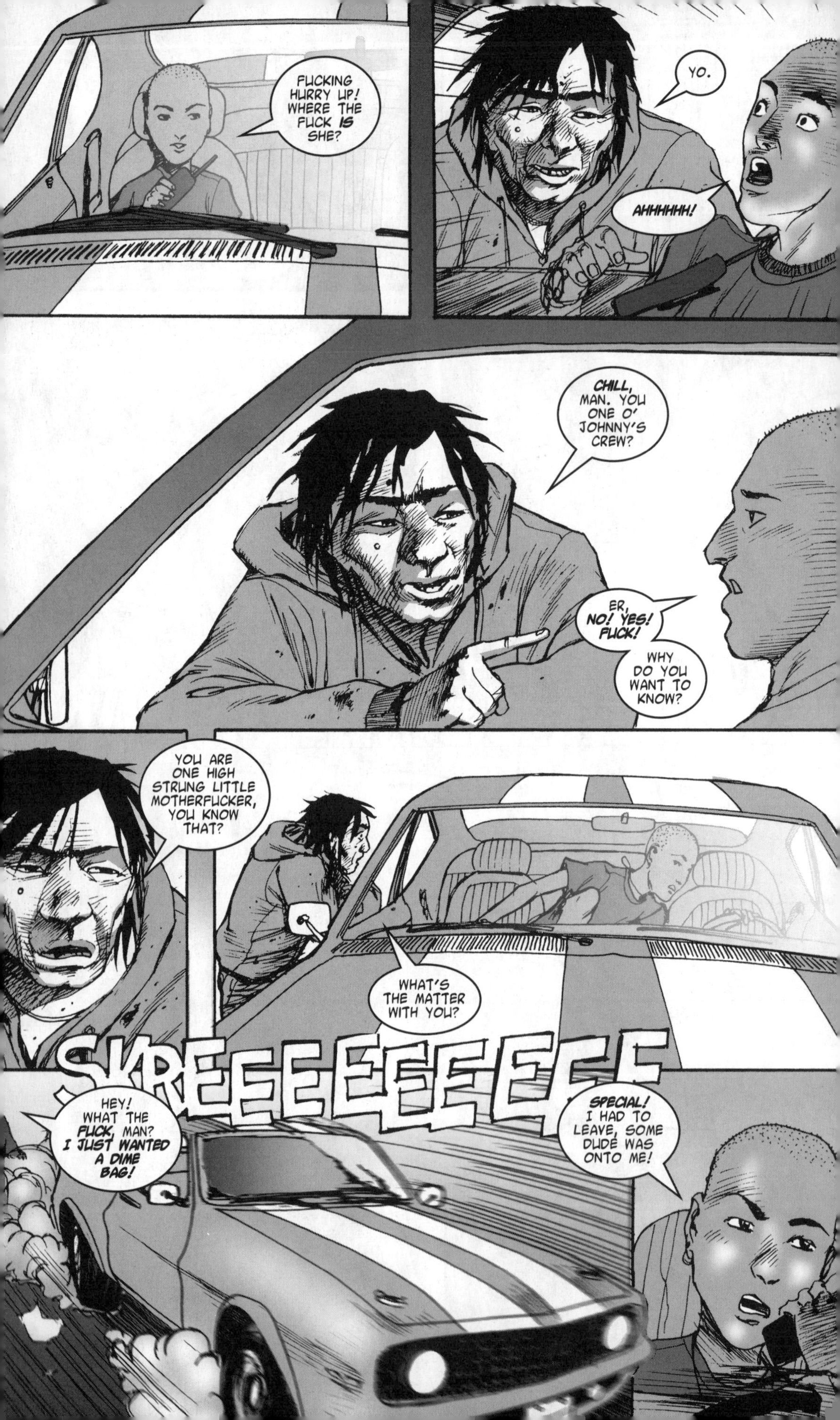
FUCKING HURRY UP! WHERE THE FUCK IS SHE?
YO.
AHHHHHH!
CHILL, MAN. YOU ONE O' JOHNNY'S CREW?
ER, NO! YES! FUCK!
WHY DO YOU WANT TO KNOW?
YOU ARE ONE HIGH STRUNG LITTLE MOTHERFUCKER, YOU KNOW THAT?
WHAT'S THE MATTER WITH YOU?
SKREEEEEEEEE
HEY! WHAT THE FUCK, MAN? I JUST WANTED A DIME BAG!
SPECIAL! I HAD TO LEAVE, SOME DUDE WAS ONTO ME!

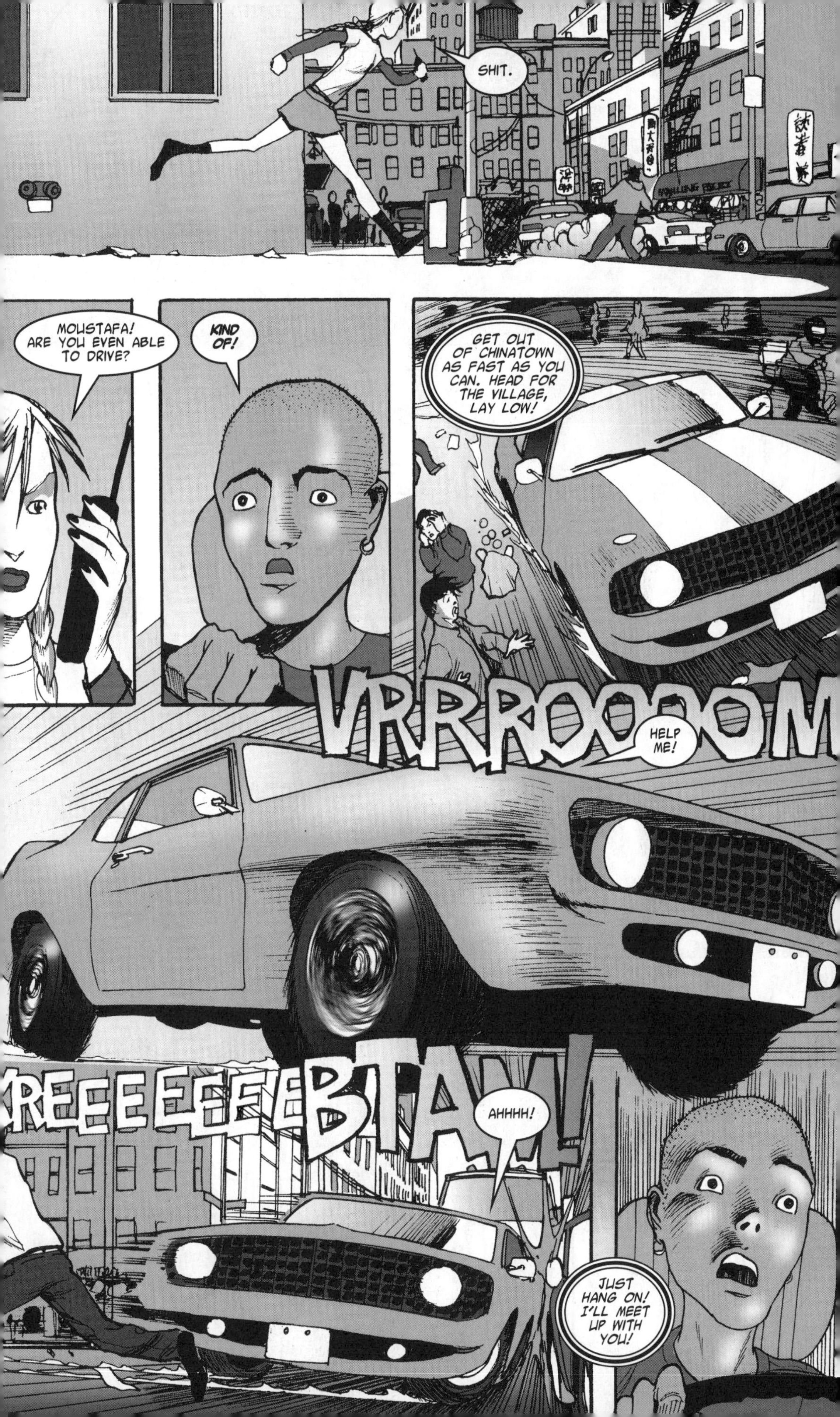
SHIT.
MOUSTAFA! ARE YOU EVEN ABLE TO DRIVE?
KIND OF!
GET OUT OF CHINATOWN AS FAST AS YOU CAN. HEAD FOR THE VILLAGE, LAY LOW!
VRRROOOOOM
HELP ME!
REEEEEEEBTAM!
AHHHH!
JUST HANG ON! I'LL MEET UP WITH YOU!

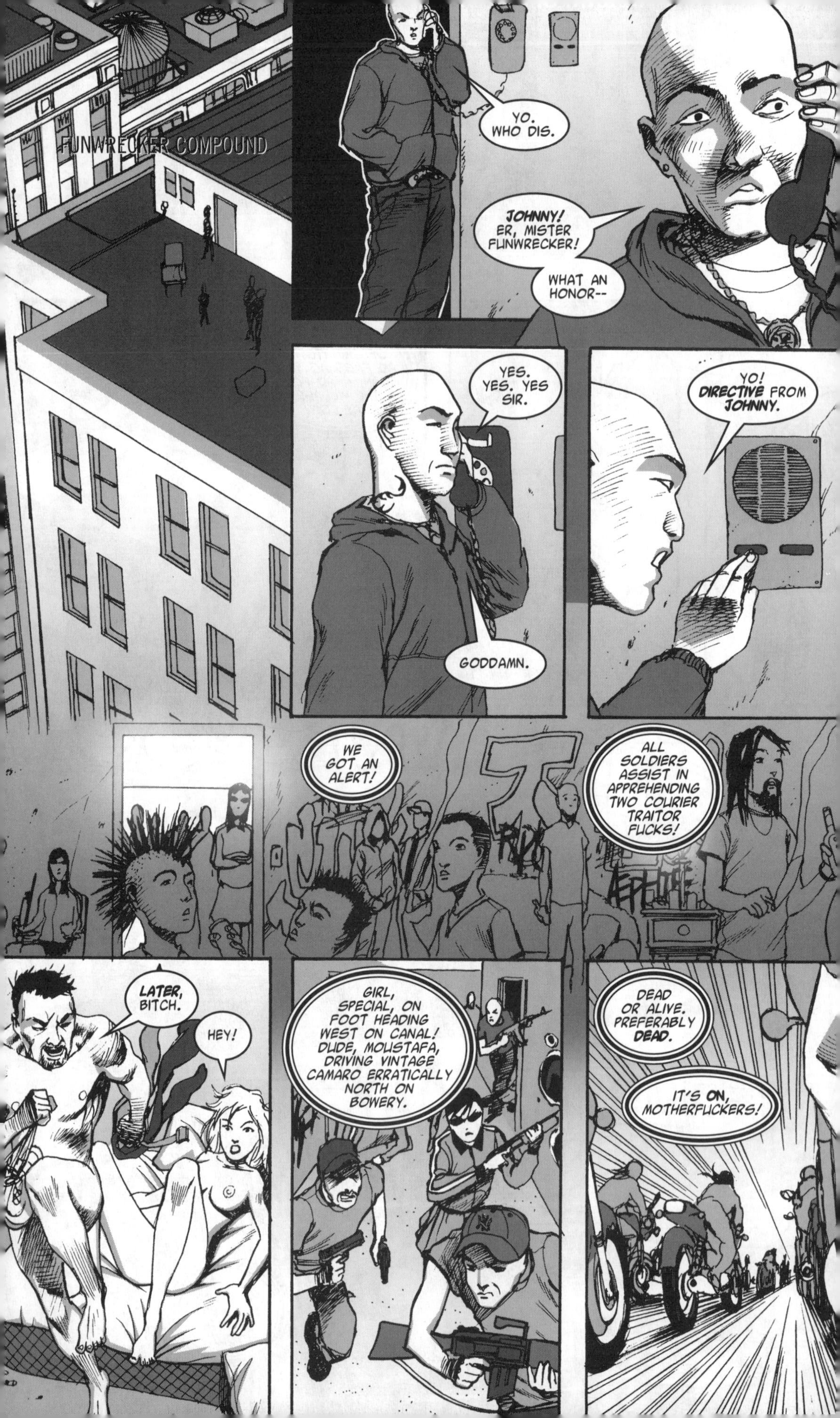
FUNWRECKER COMPOUND
YO. WHO DIS.
JOHNNY! ER, MISTER FUNWRECKER!
WHAT AN HONOR--
YES. YES. YES SIR.
GODDAMN.
YO! DIRECTIVE FROM JOHNNY.
WE GOT AN ALERT!
ALL SOLDIERS ASSIST IN APPREHENDING TWO COURIER TRAITOR FUCKS!
LATER, BITCH.
HEY!
GIRL, SPECIAL, ON FOOT HEADING WEST ON CANAL! DUDE, MOUSTAFA, DRIVING VINTAGE CAMARO ERRATICALLY NORTH ON BOWERY.
DEAD OR ALIVE. PREFERABLY DEAD.
IT'S ON, MOTHERFUCKERS!

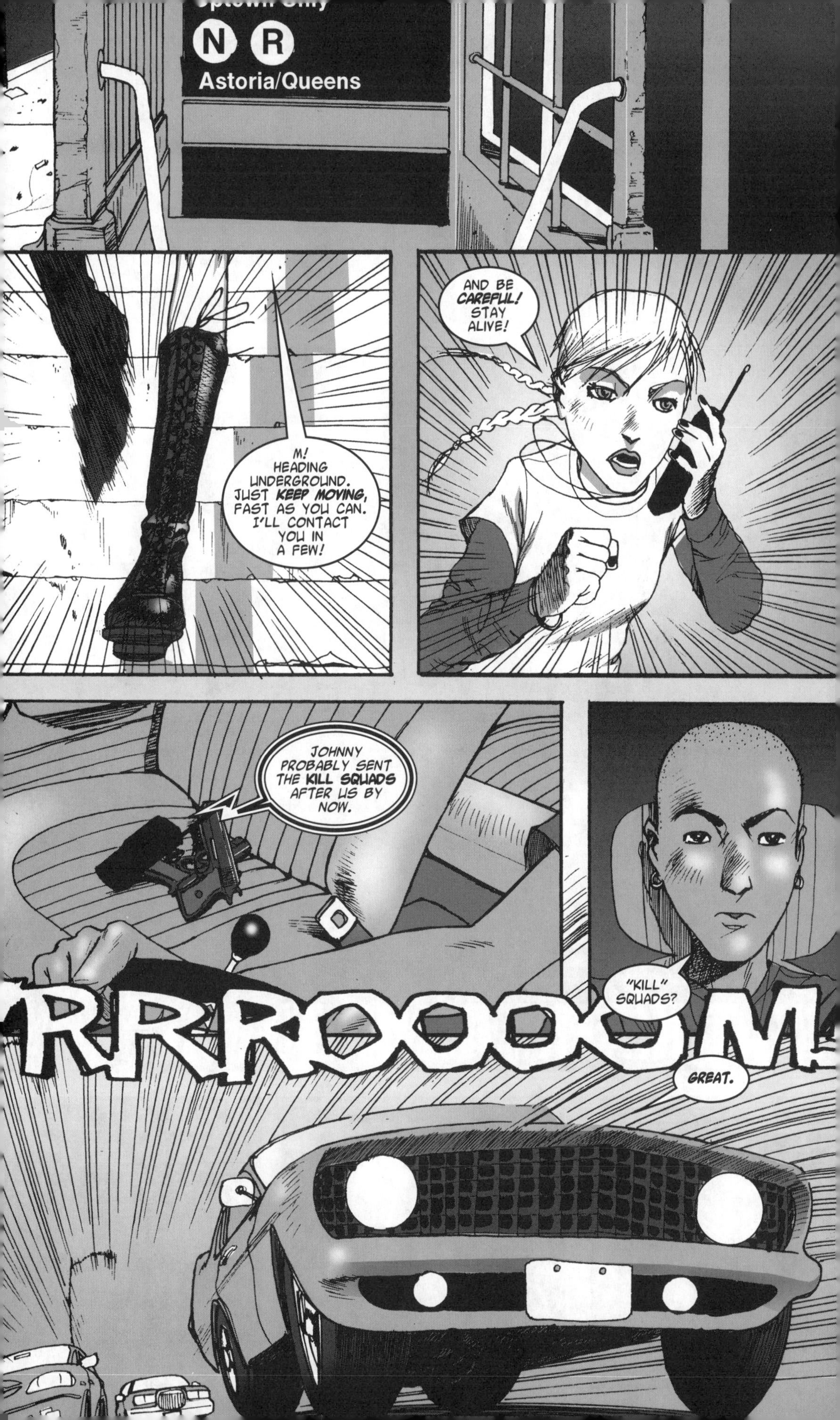
Uptown Only
N R
Astoria/Queens
M! HEADING UNDERGROUND. JUST KEEP MOVING, FAST AS YOU CAN. I'LL CONTACT YOU IN A FEW!
AND BE CAREFUL! STAY ALIVE!
JOHNNY PROBABLY SENT THE KILL SQUADS AFTER US BY NOW.
"KILL" SQUADS?
RRROOOOM!
GREAT.

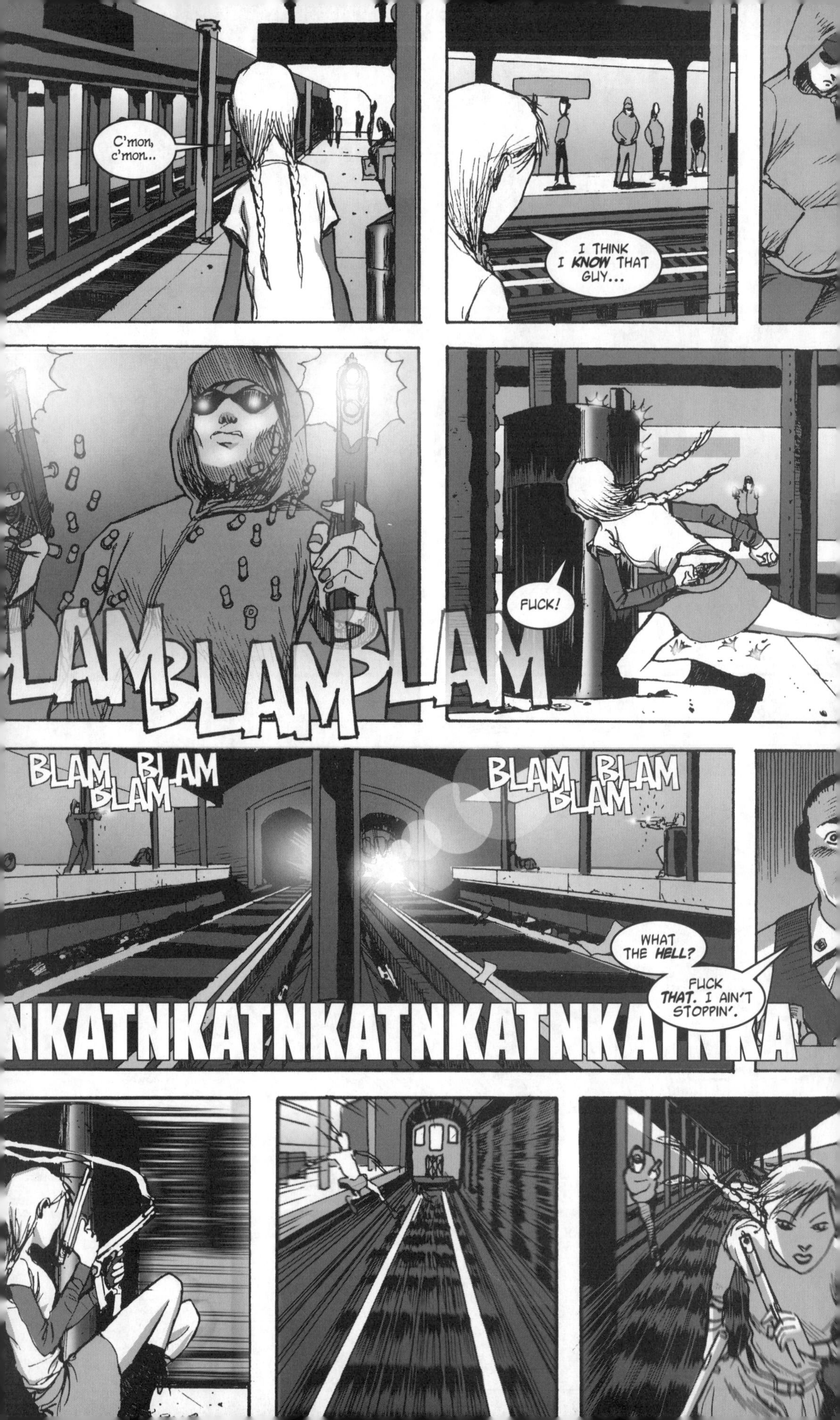
C'mon, c'mon...
I THINK I **KNOW** THAT GUY...
BLAMBLAMBLAM
FUCK!
BLAM BLAM BLAM
BLAM BLAM BLAM
WHAT THE **HELL?**
FUCK **THAT.** I AIN'T STOPPIN'.
NKATNKATNKATNKATNKATNKA

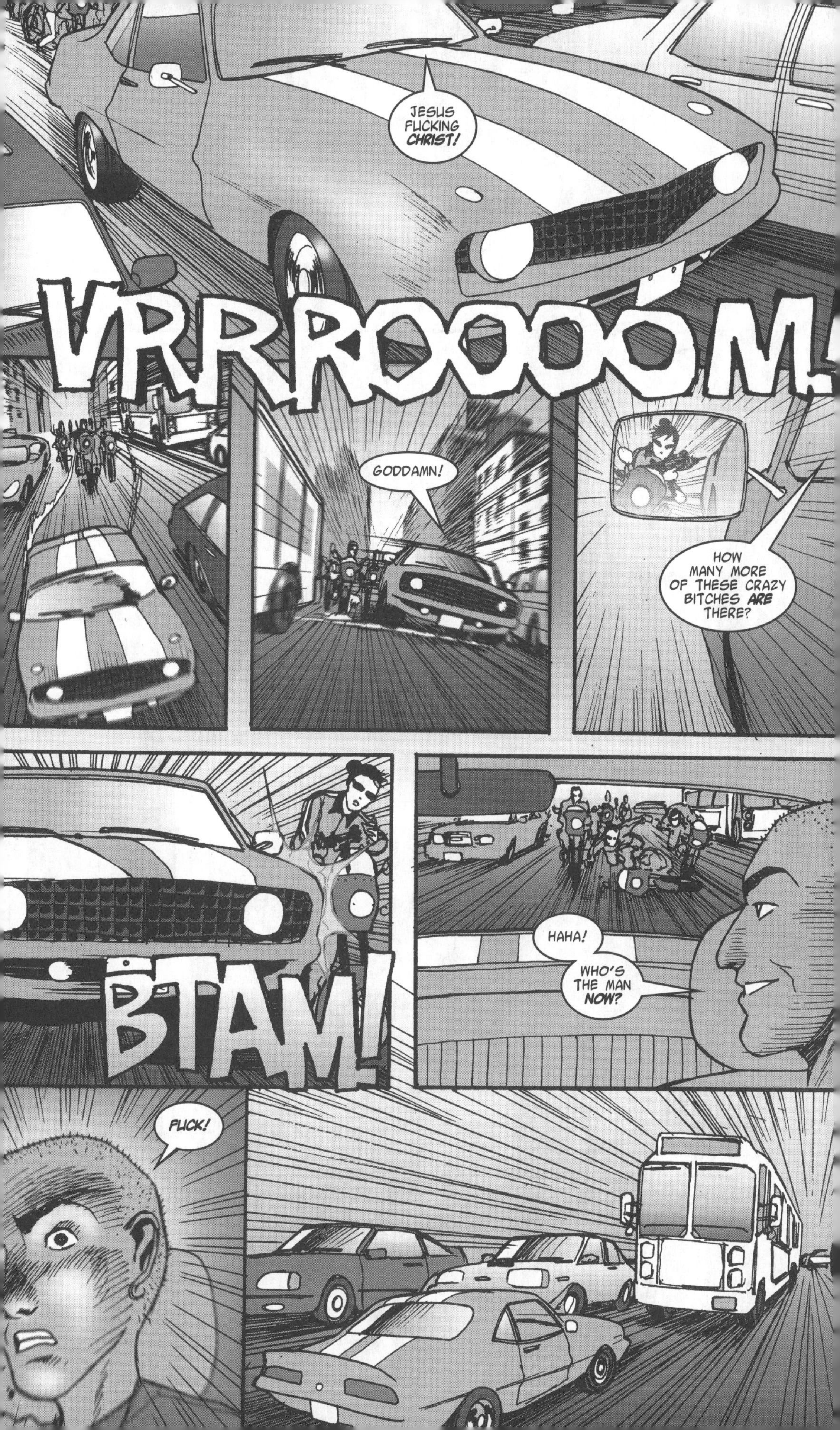
JESUS FUCKING CHRIST!
VRRROOOOM!
GODDAMN!
HOW MANY MORE OF THESE CRAZY BITCHES ARE THERE?
BTAM!
HAHA!
WHO'S THE MAN NOW?
FUCK!

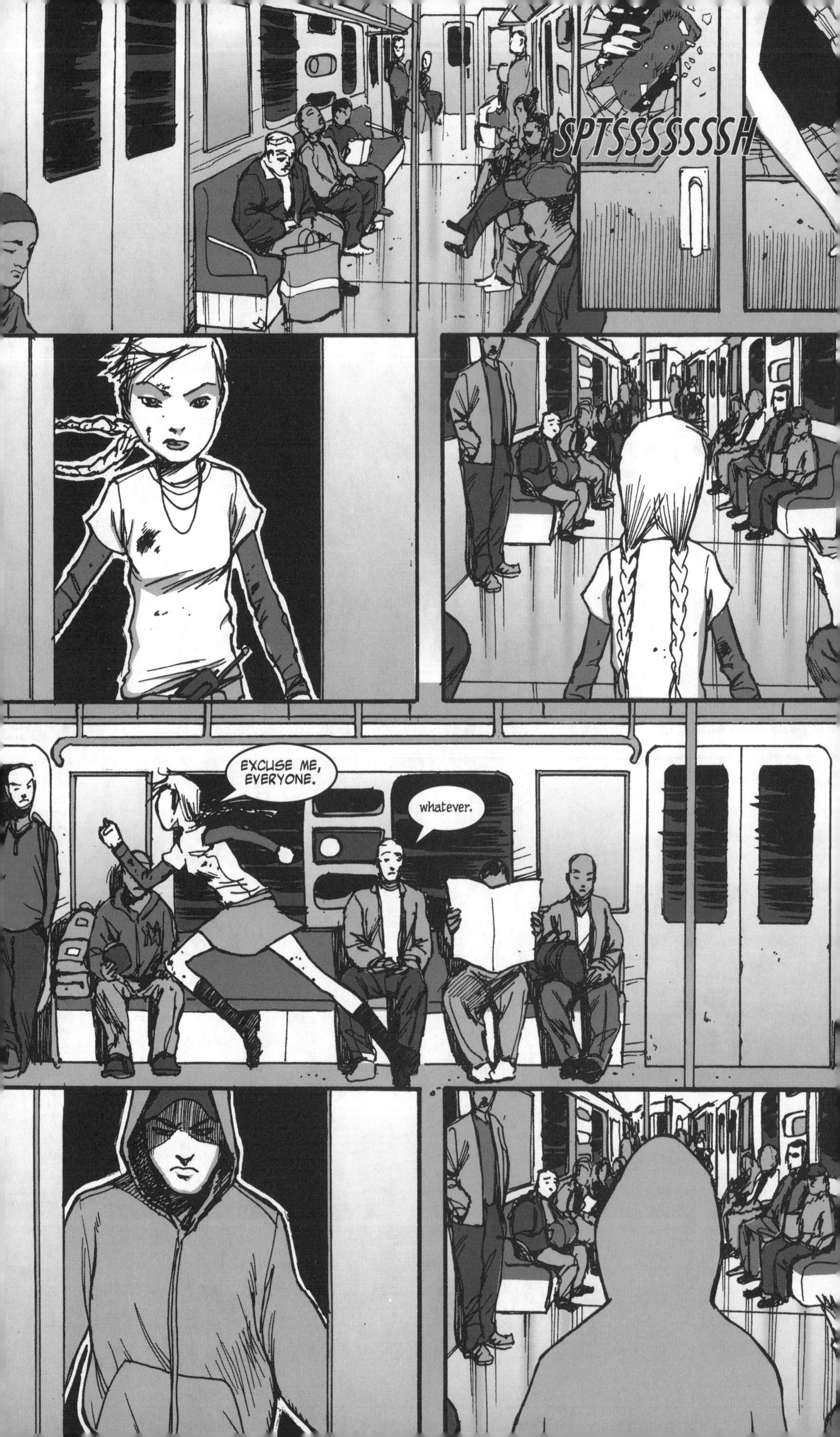
SPTSSSSSSSH
EXCUSE ME, EVERYONE.
whatever.

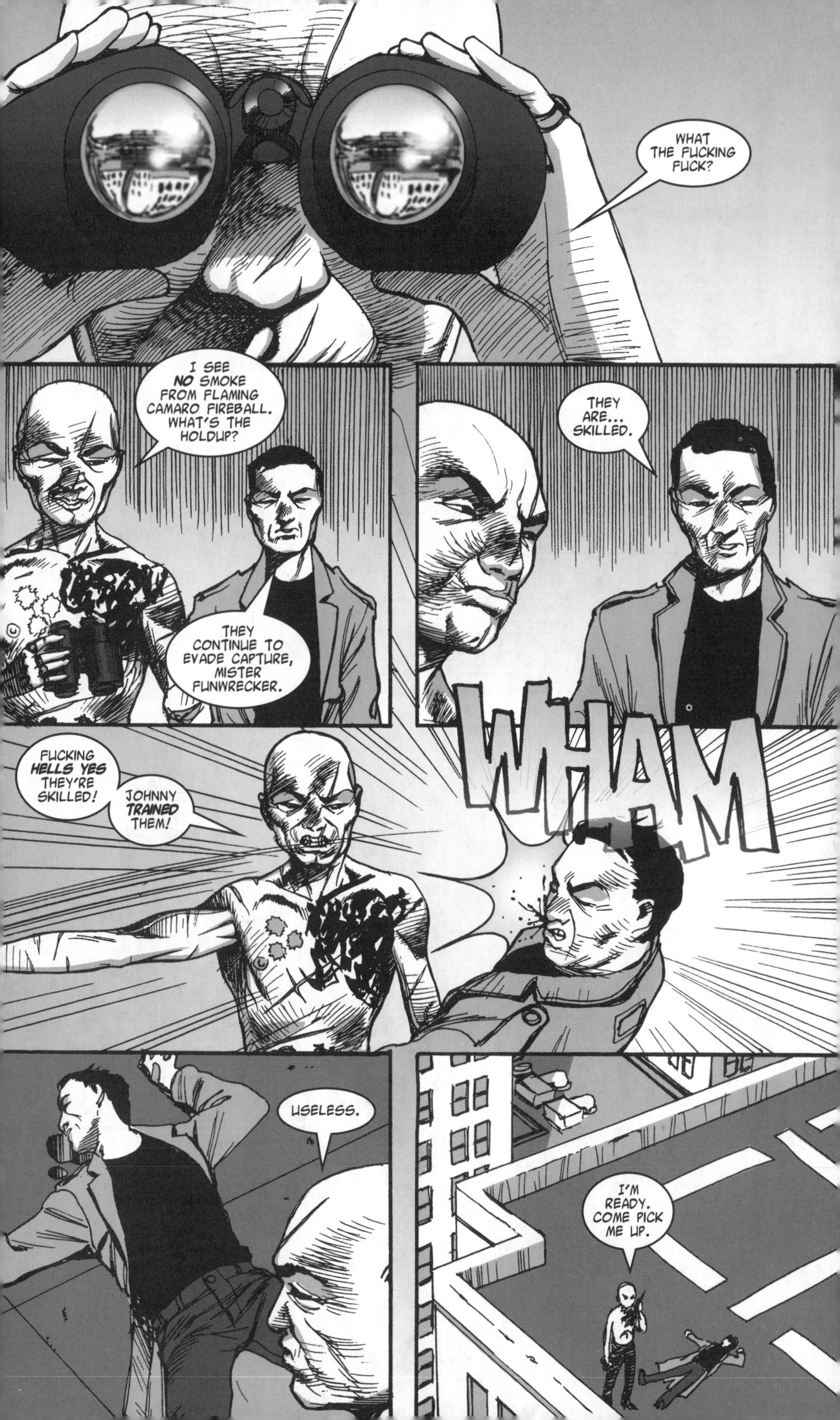

WHAT THE FUCKING FUCK?
I SEE **NO** SMOKE FROM FLAMING CAMARO FIREBALL. WHAT'S THE HOLDUP?
THEY CONTINUE TO EVADE CAPTURE, MISTER FUNWRECKER.
THEY ARE... SKILLED.
WHAM
FUCKING **HELLS YES** THEY'RE SKILLED!
JOHNNY **TRAINED** THEM!
USELESS.
I'M READY. COME PICK ME UP.

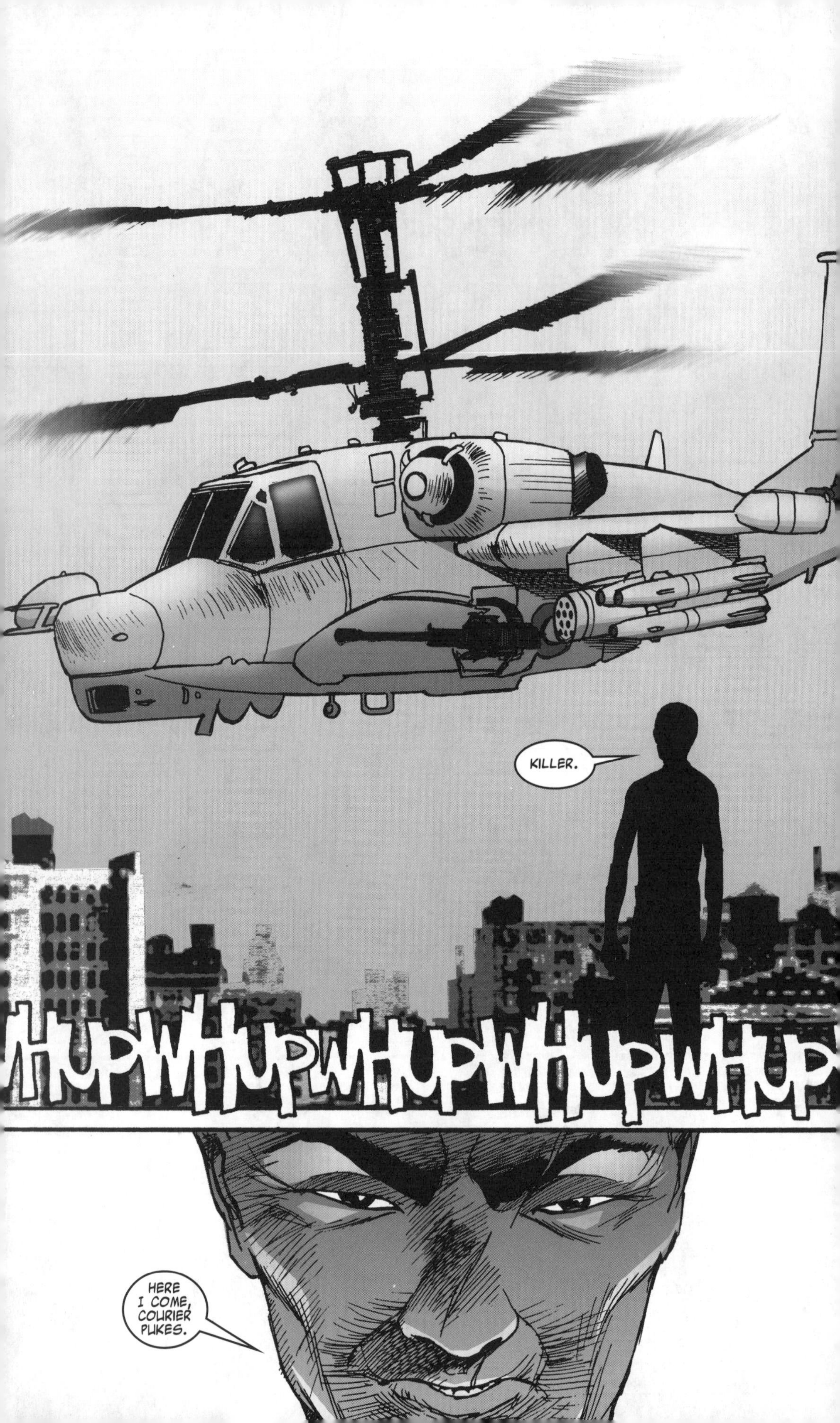
KILLER.
WHUPWHUPWHUPWHUPWHUP
HERE I COME, COURIER PUKES.

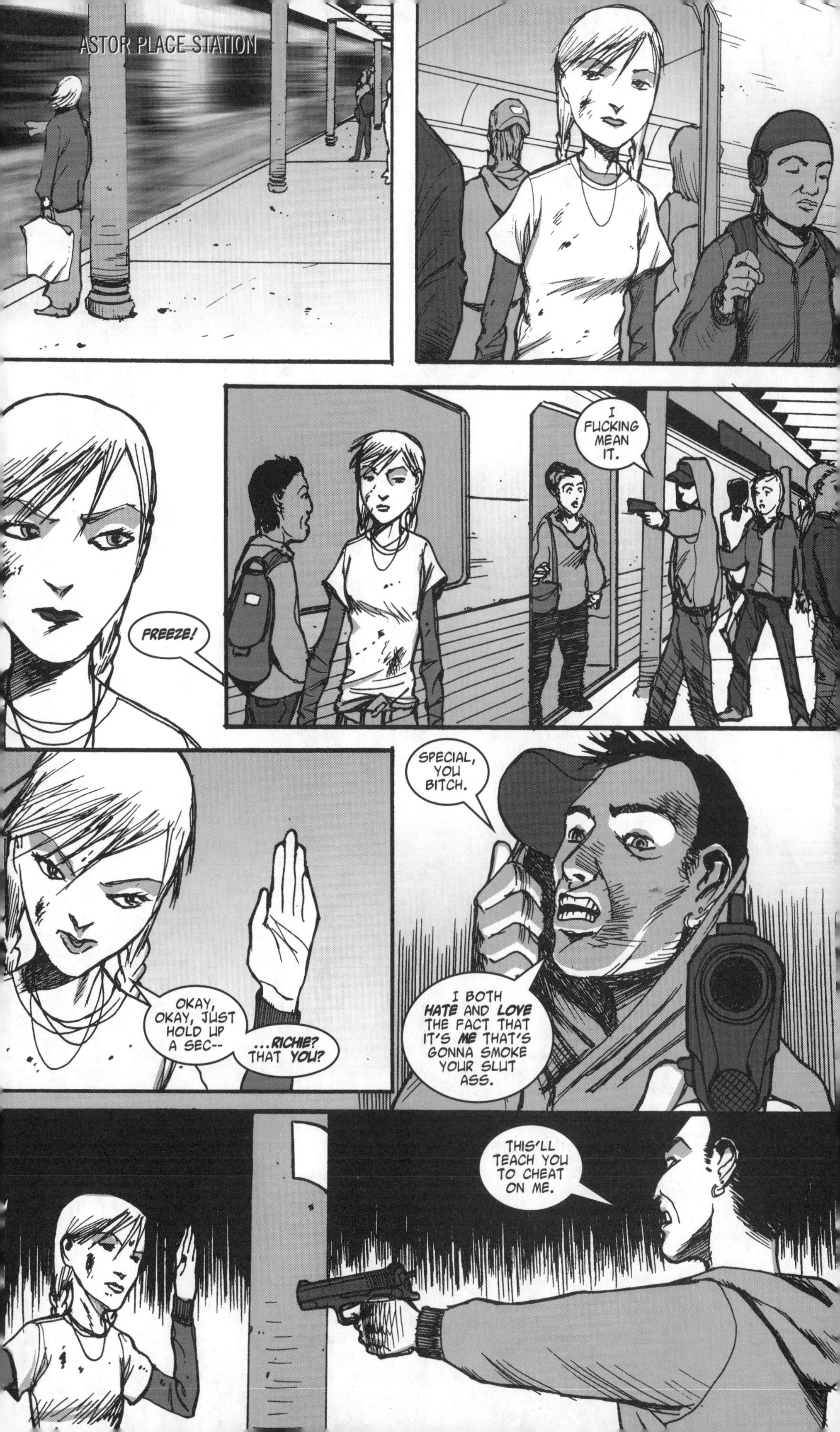
ASTOR PLACE STATION
I FUCKING MEAN IT.
FREEZE!
SPECIAL, YOU BITCH.
OKAY, OKAY, JUST HOLD UP A SEC--
...RICHIE? THAT YOU?
I BOTH HATE AND LOVE THE FACT THAT IT'S ME THAT'S GONNA SMOKE YOUR SLUT ASS.
THIS'LL TEACH YOU TO CHEAT ON ME.

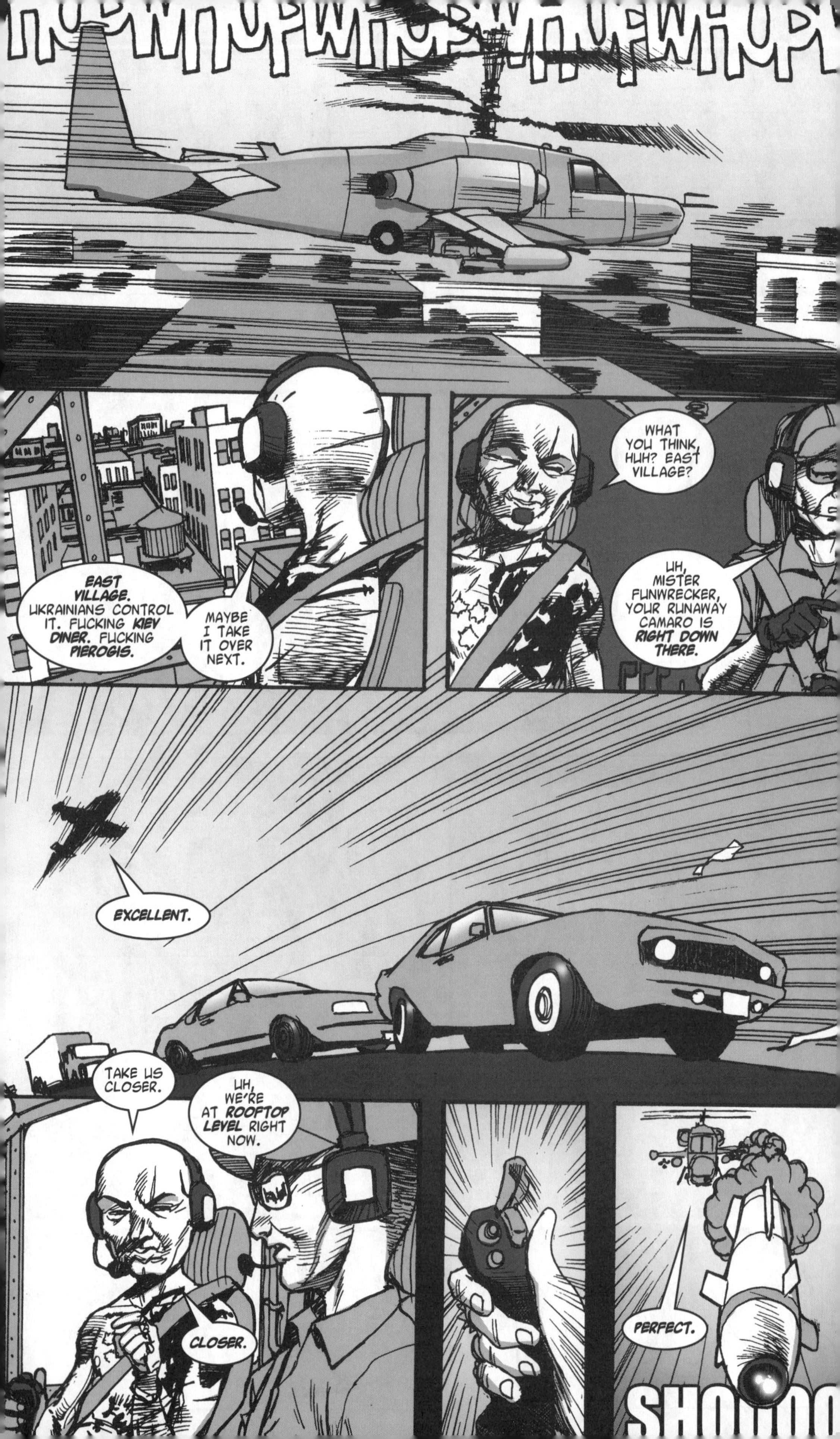

EAST VILLAGE. UKRAINIANS CONTROL IT. FUCKING KIEV DINER. FUCKING PIEROGIS.
MAYBE I TAKE IT OVER NEXT.
WHAT YOU THINK, HUH? EAST VILLAGE?
UH, MISTER FUNWRECKER, YOUR RUNAWAY CAMARO IS RIGHT DOWN THERE.
EXCELLENT.
TAKE US CLOSER.
UH, WE'RE AT ROOFTOP LEVEL RIGHT NOW.
CLOSER.
PERFECT.

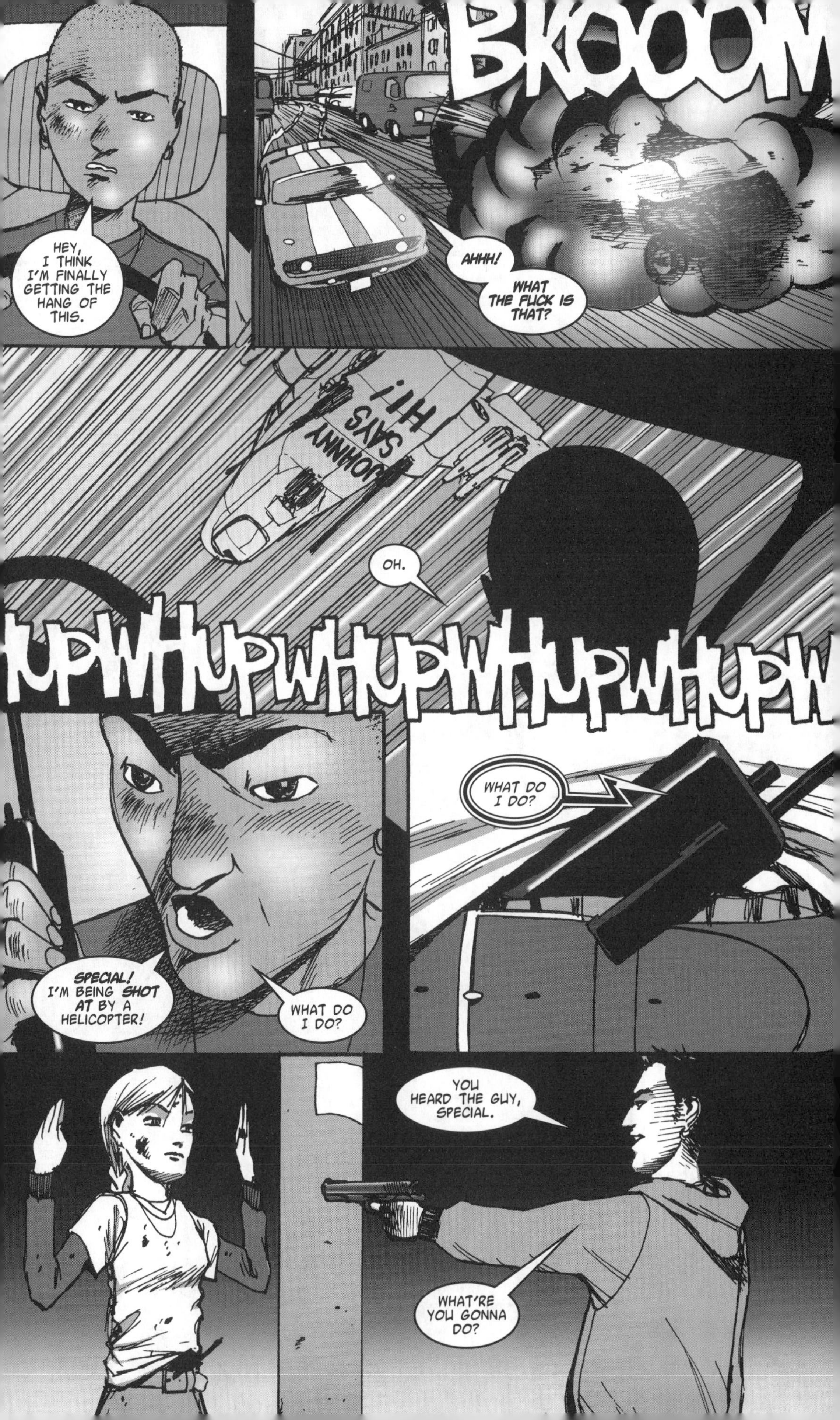
HEY, I THINK I'M FINALLY GETTING THE HANG OF THIS.
BKOOOM
AHHH!
WHAT THE FUCK IS THAT?
JOHNNY SAYS HI!
OH.
UPWHUPWHUPWHUPWHUPW
SPECIAL! I'M BEING SHOT AT BY A HELICOPTER!
WHAT DO I DO?
WHAT DO I DO?
YOU HEARD THE GUY, SPECIAL.
WHAT'RE YOU GONNA DO?

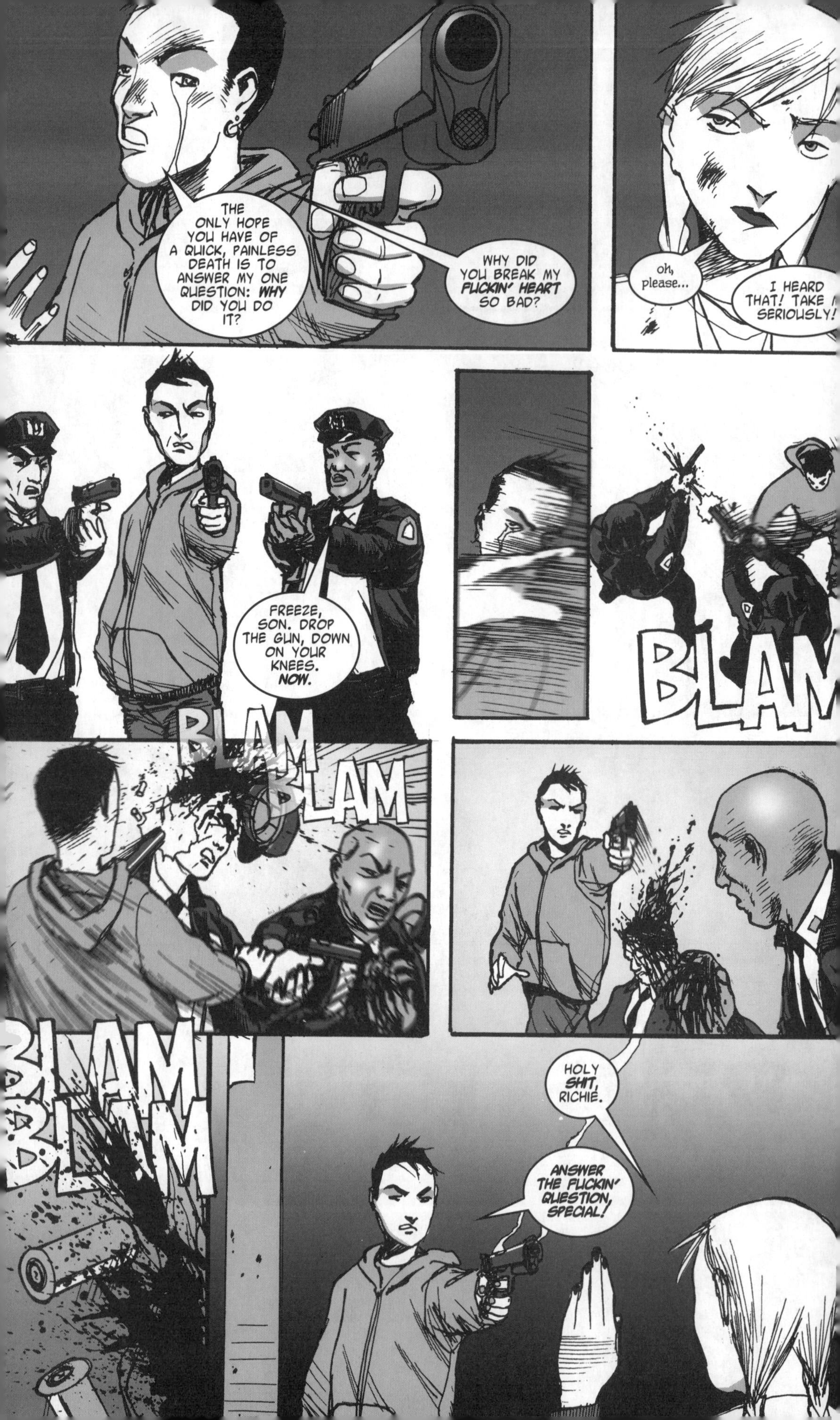
THE ONLY HOPE YOU HAVE OF A QUICK, PAINLESS DEATH IS TO ANSWER MY ONE QUESTION: WHY DID YOU DO IT?
WHY DID YOU BREAK MY FUCKIN' HEART SO BAD?
oh, please...
I HEARD THAT! TAKE SERIOUSLY!
FREEZE, SON. DROP THE GUN, DOWN ON YOUR KNEES. NOW.
BLAM
BLAM
BLAM
BLAM
BLAM
HOLY SHIT, RICHIE.
ANSWER THE FUCKIN' QUESTION, SPECIAL!

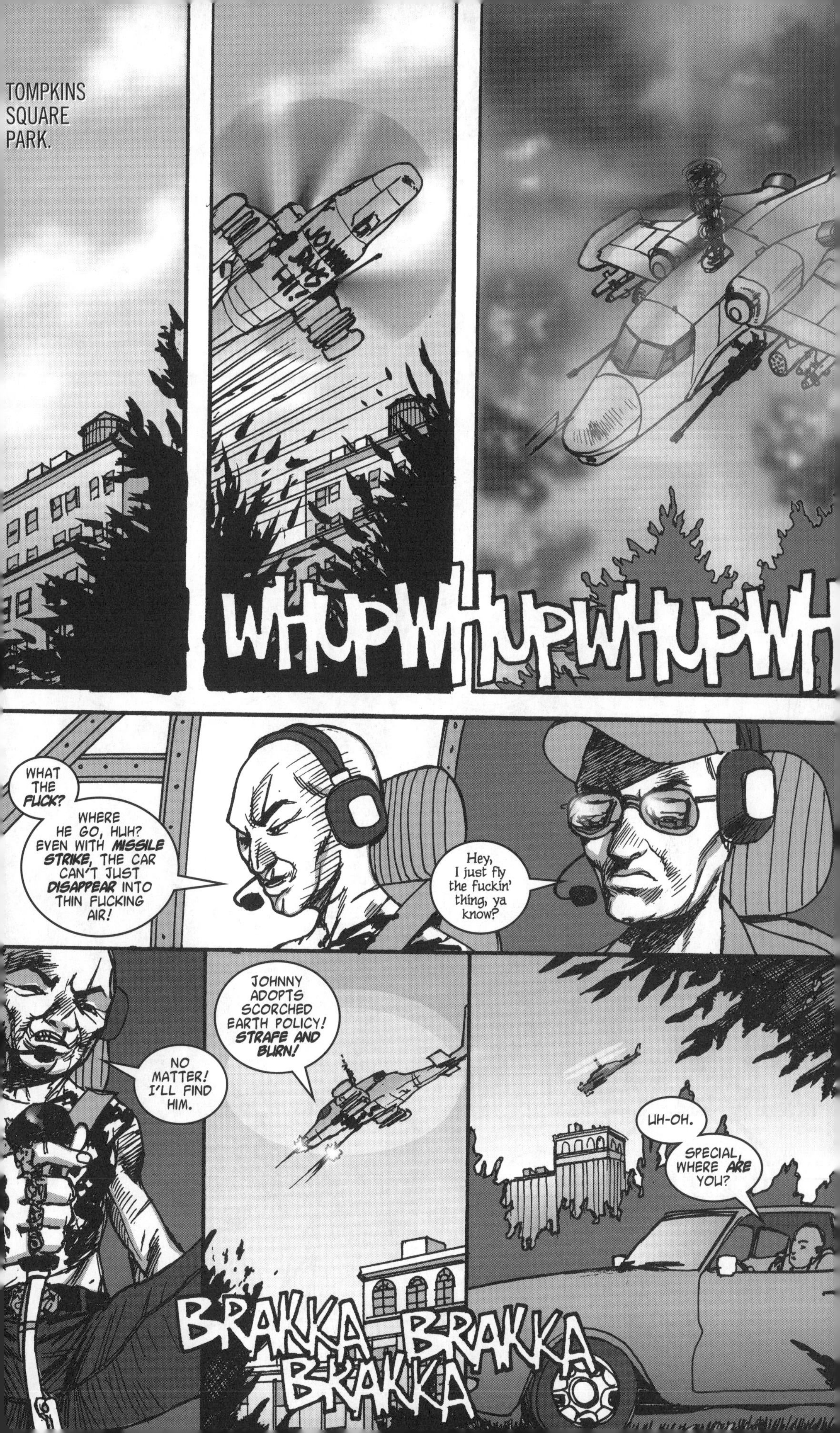
TOMPKINS SQUARE PARK.
WHUPWHUPWHUPWH
WHAT THE FUCK?
WHERE HE GO, HUH? EVEN WITH MISSILE STRIKE, THE CAR CAN'T JUST DISAPPEAR INTO THIN FUCKING AIR!
Hey, I just fly the fuckin' thing, ya know?
NO MATTER! I'LL FIND HIM.
JOHNNY ADOPTS SCORCHED EARTH POLICY! STRAFE AND BURN!
UH-OH.
SPECIAL, WHERE ARE YOU?
BRAKKA BRAKKA BRAKKA

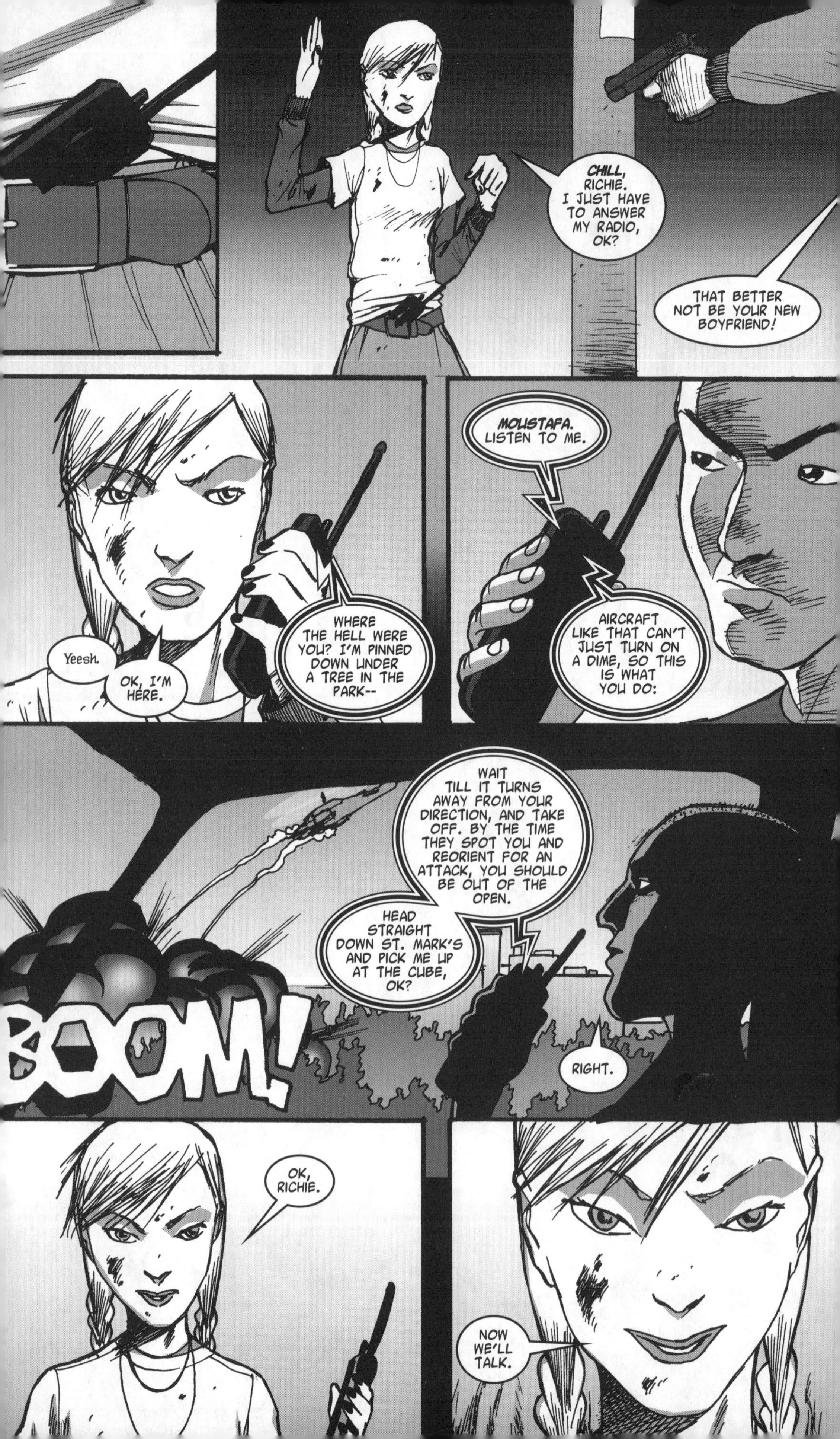
CHILL, RICHIE. I JUST HAVE TO ANSWER MY RADIO, OK?
THAT BETTER NOT BE YOUR NEW BOYFRIEND!
Yeesh.
OK, I'M HERE.
WHERE THE HELL WERE YOU? I'M PINNED DOWN UNDER A TREE IN THE PARK--
MOUSTAFA. LISTEN TO ME.
AIRCRAFT LIKE THAT CAN'T JUST TURN ON A DIME, SO THIS IS WHAT YOU DO:
WAIT TILL IT TURNS AWAY FROM YOUR DIRECTION, AND TAKE OFF. BY THE TIME THEY SPOT YOU AND REORIENT FOR AN ATTACK, YOU SHOULD BE OUT OF THE OPEN.
HEAD STRAIGHT DOWN ST. MARK'S AND PICK ME UP AT THE CUBE, OK?
BOOM!
RIGHT.
OK, RICHIE.
NOW WE'LL TALK.

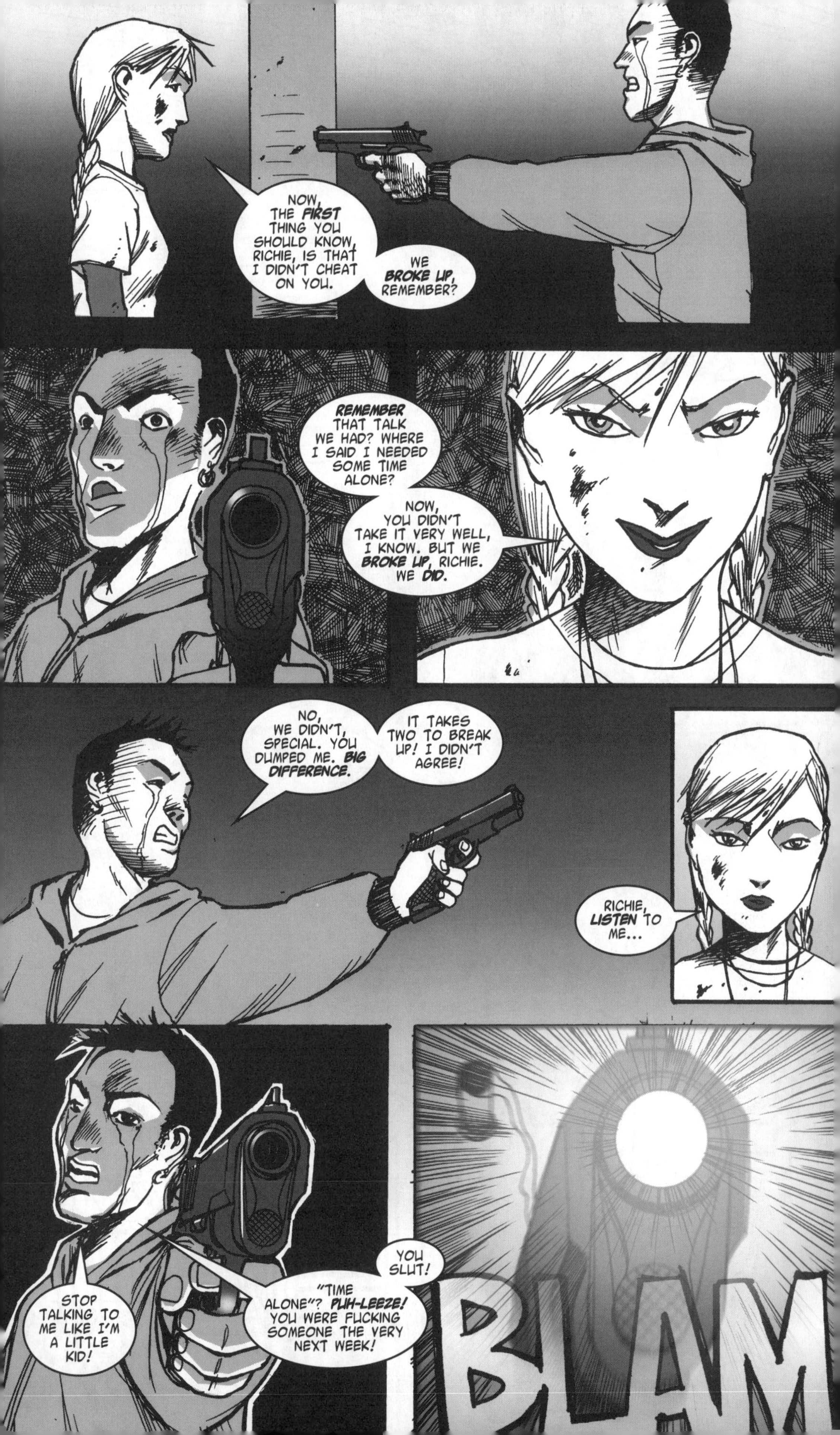
NOW, THE FIRST THING YOU SHOULD KNOW, RICHIE, IS THAT I DIDN'T CHEAT ON YOU.
WE BROKE UP, REMEMBER?
REMEMBER THAT TALK WE HAD? WHERE I SAID I NEEDED SOME TIME ALONE?
NOW, YOU DIDN'T TAKE IT VERY WELL, I KNOW. BUT WE BROKE UP, RICHIE. WE DID.
NO, WE DIDN'T, SPECIAL. YOU DUMPED ME. BIG DIFFERENCE.
IT TAKES TWO TO BREAK UP! I DIDN'T AGREE!
RICHIE, LISTEN TO ME...
STOP TALKING TO ME LIKE I'M A LITTLE KID!
"TIME ALONE"? PUH-LEEZE! YOU WERE FUCKING SOMEONE THE VERY NEXT WEEK!
YOU SLUT!
BLAM

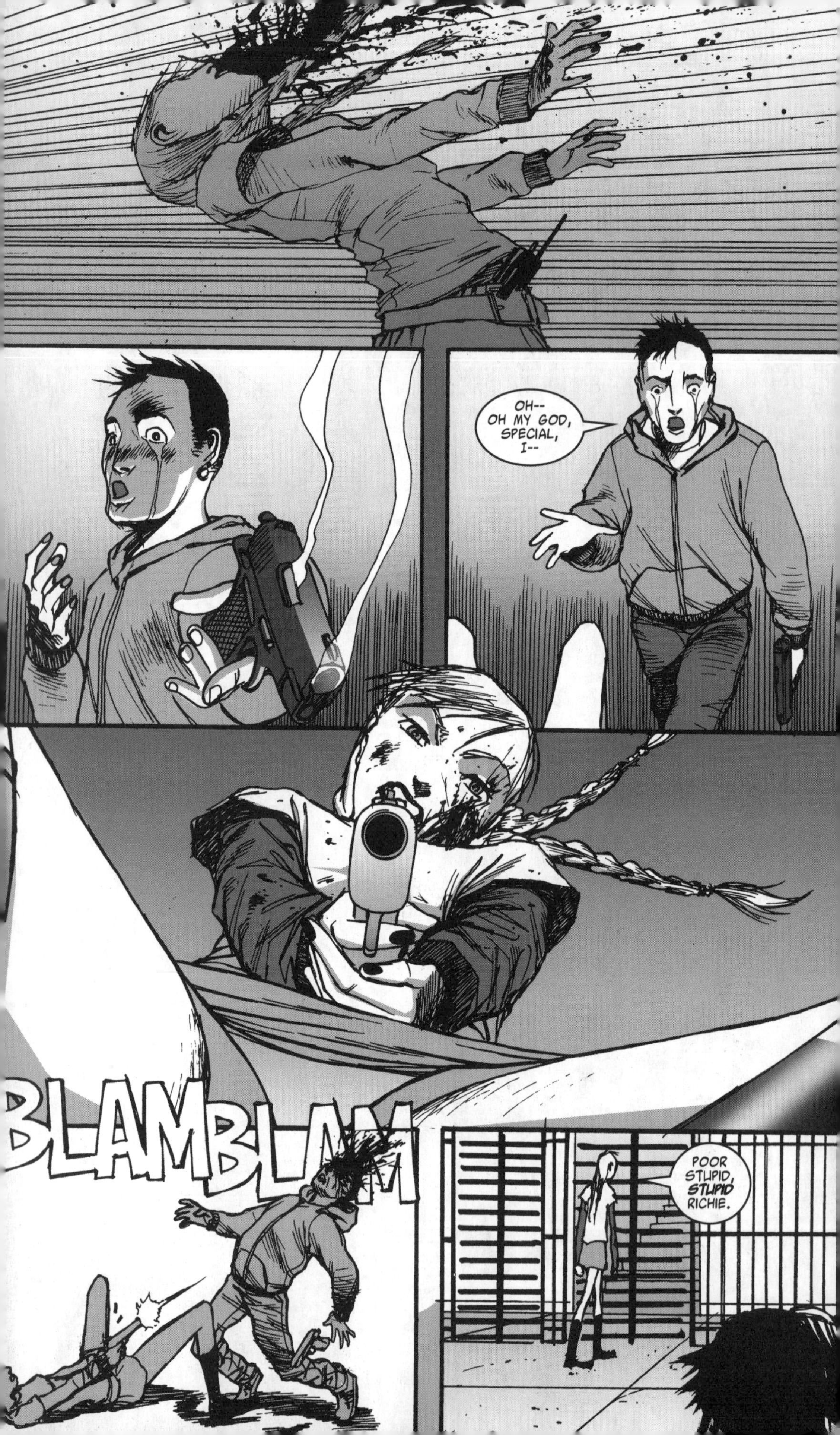
OH--
OH MY GOD, SPECIAL, I--
BLAMBLAM
POOR STUPID, *STUPID* RICHIE.

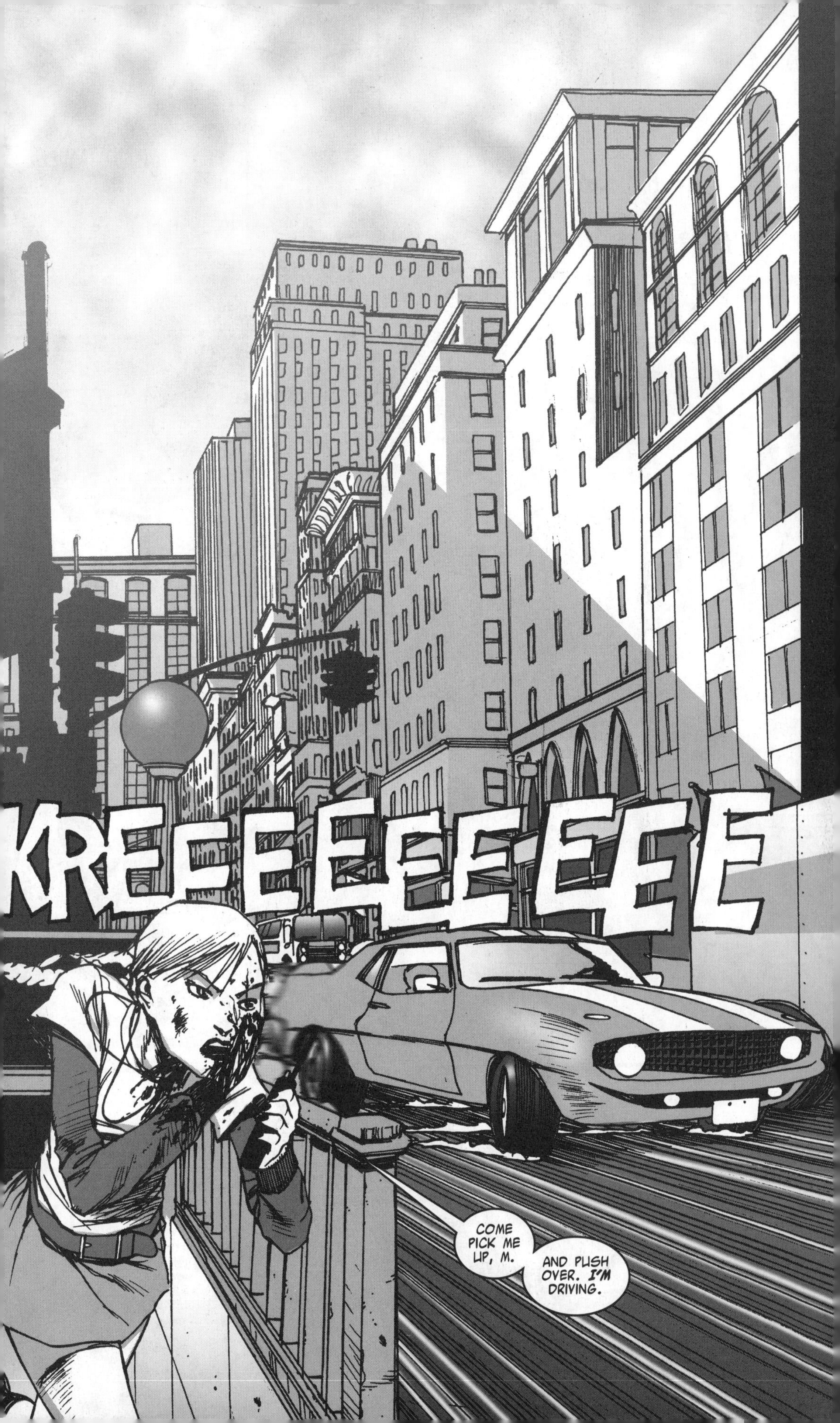
KREEEEEEEEE
COME PICK ME UP, M.
AND PUSH OVER. I'M DRIVING.

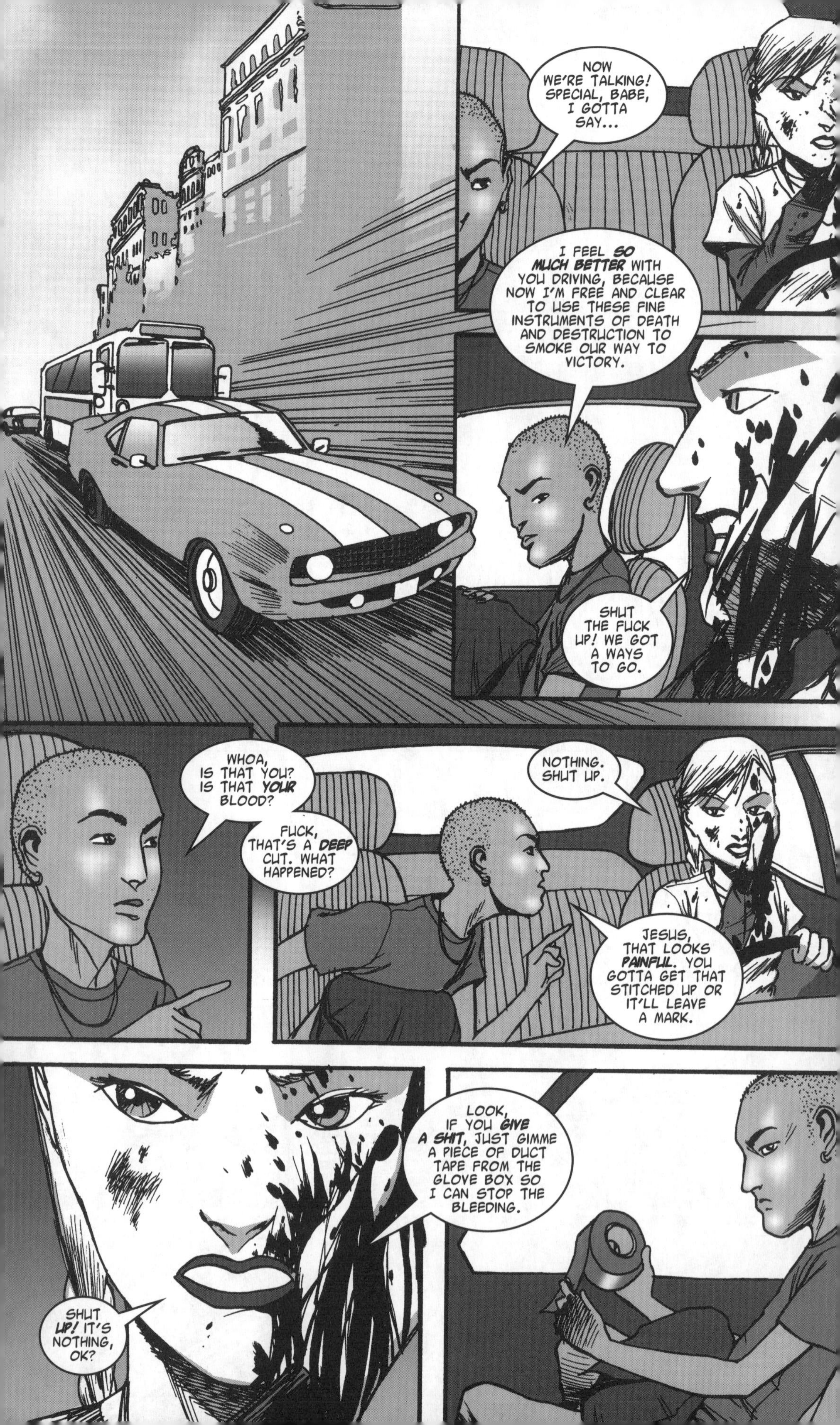
NOW WE'RE TALKING! SPECIAL, BABE, I GOTTA SAY...
I FEEL **SO MUCH BETTER** WITH YOU DRIVING, BECAUSE NOW I'M FREE AND CLEAR TO USE THESE FINE INSTRUMENTS OF DEATH AND DESTRUCTION TO SMOKE OUR WAY TO VICTORY.
SHUT THE FUCK UP! WE GOT A WAYS TO GO.
WHOA, IS THAT YOU? IS THAT **YOUR** BLOOD?
FUCK, THAT'S A **DEEP** CUT. WHAT HAPPENED?
NOTHING. SHUT UP.
JESUS, THAT LOOKS **PAINFUL**. YOU GOTTA GET THAT STITCHED UP OR IT'LL LEAVE A MARK.
SHUT **UP!** IT'S NOTHING, OK?
LOOK, IF YOU **GIVE A SHIT**, JUST GIMME A PIECE OF DUCT TAPE FROM THE GLOVE BOX SO I CAN STOP THE BLEEDING.

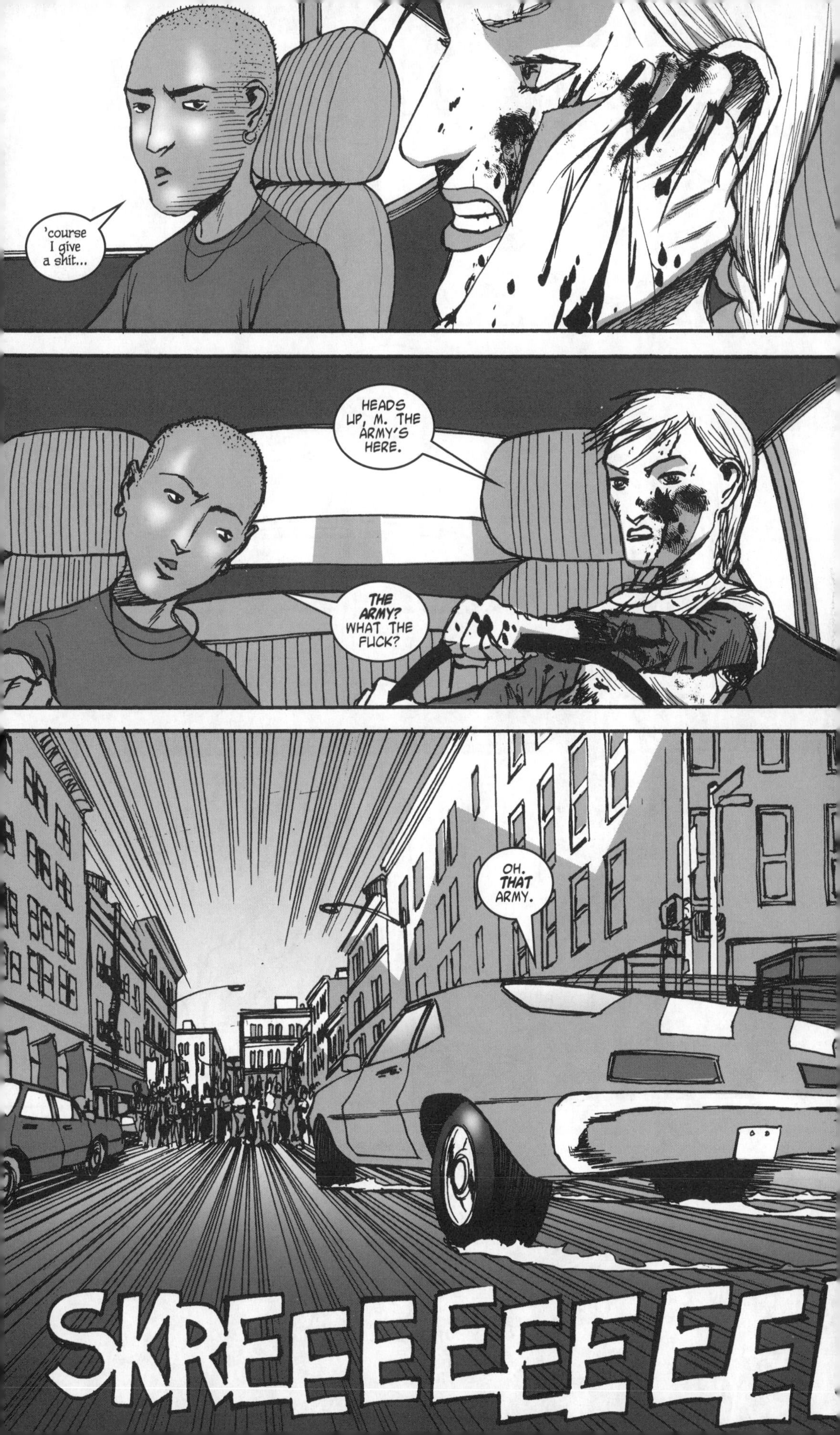
'course I give a shit...
HEADS UP, M. THE ARMY'S HERE.
THE ARMY? WHAT THE FUCK?
OH. THAT ARMY.
SKREEEEEEEEEE

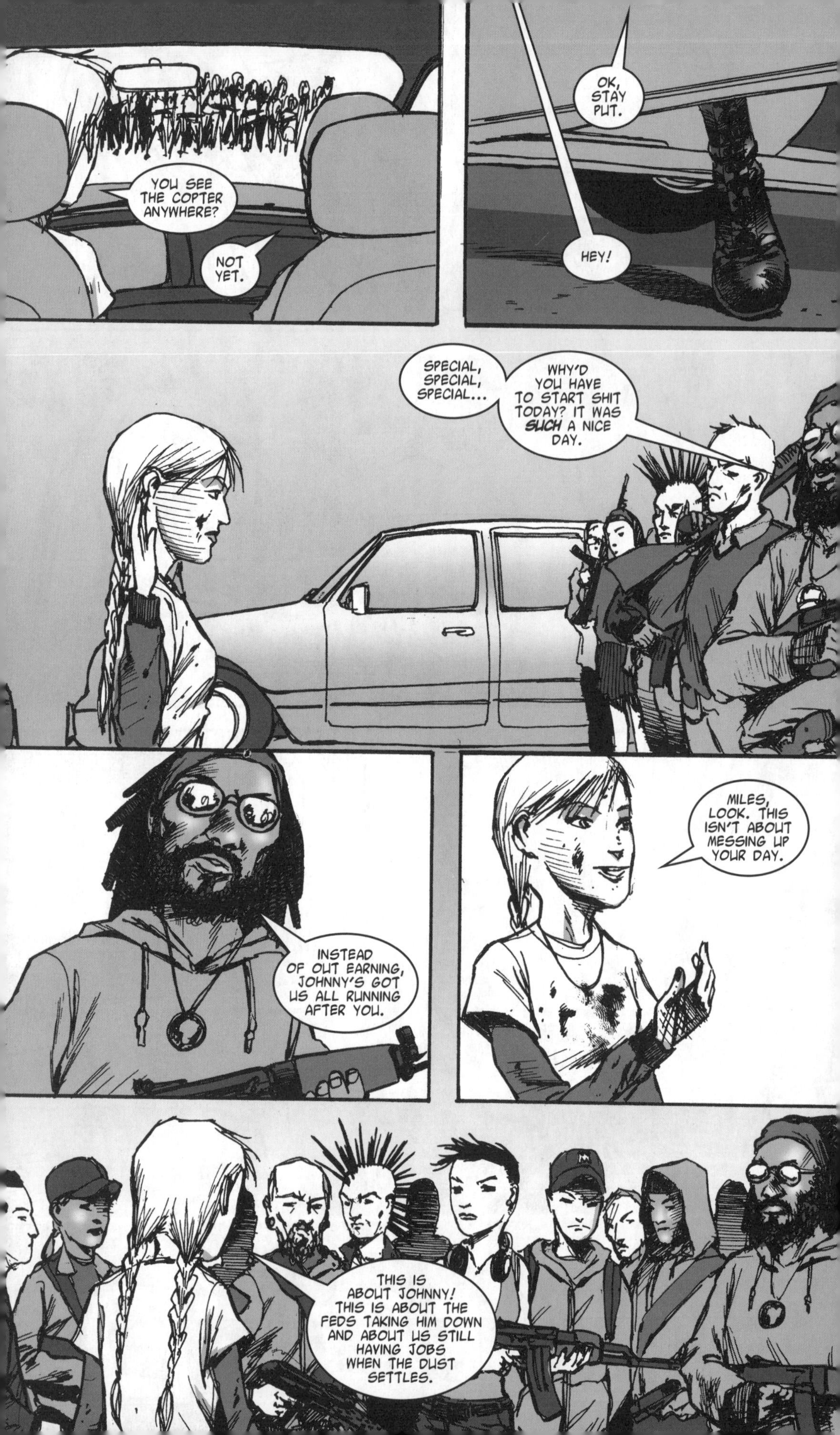
YOU SEE THE COPTER ANYWHERE?
NOT YET.
OK, STAY PUT.
HEY!
SPECIAL, SPECIAL, SPECIAL...
WHY'D YOU HAVE TO START SHIT TODAY? IT WAS *SUCH* A NICE DAY.
INSTEAD OF OUT EARNING, JOHNNY'S GOT US ALL RUNNING AFTER YOU.
MILES, LOOK. THIS ISN'T ABOUT MESSING UP YOUR DAY.
THIS IS ABOUT JOHNNY! THIS IS ABOUT THE FEDS TAKING HIM DOWN AND ABOUT US STILL HAVING JOBS WHEN THE DUST SETTLES.

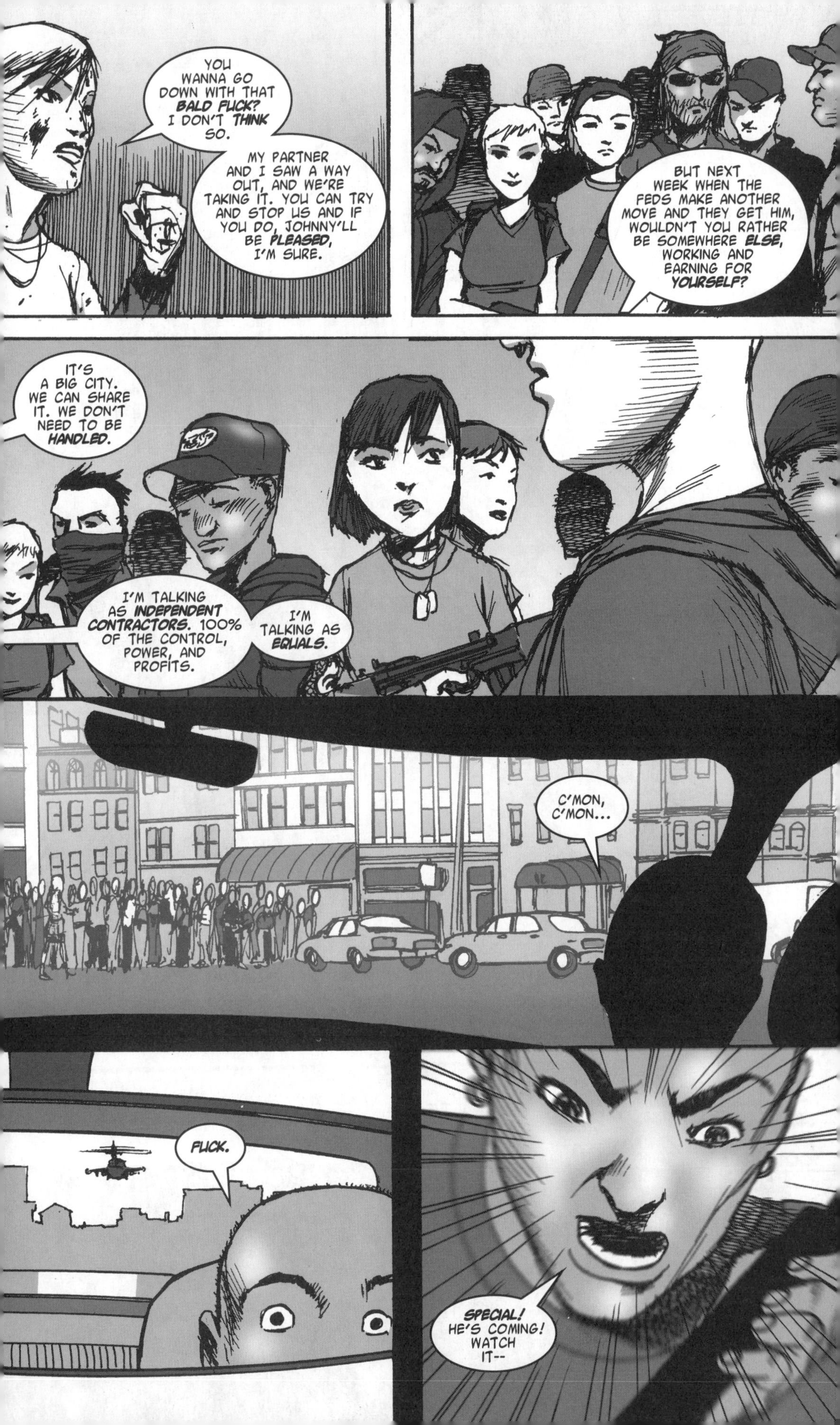
YOU WANNA GO DOWN WITH THAT BALD FUCK? I DON'T THINK SO.
MY PARTNER AND I SAW A WAY OUT, AND WE'RE TAKING IT. YOU CAN TRY AND STOP US AND IF YOU DO, JOHNNY'LL BE PLEASED, I'M SURE.
BUT NEXT WEEK WHEN THE FEDS MAKE ANOTHER MOVE AND THEY GET HIM, WOULDN'T YOU RATHER BE SOMEWHERE ELSE, WORKING AND EARNING FOR YOURSELF?
IT'S A BIG CITY. WE CAN SHARE IT. WE DON'T NEED TO BE HANDLED.
I'M TALKING AS INDEPENDENT CONTRACTORS. 100% OF THE CONTROL, POWER, AND PROFITS.
I'M TALKING AS EQUALS.
C'MON, C'MON...
FUCK.
SPECIAL! HE'S COMING! WATCH IT--

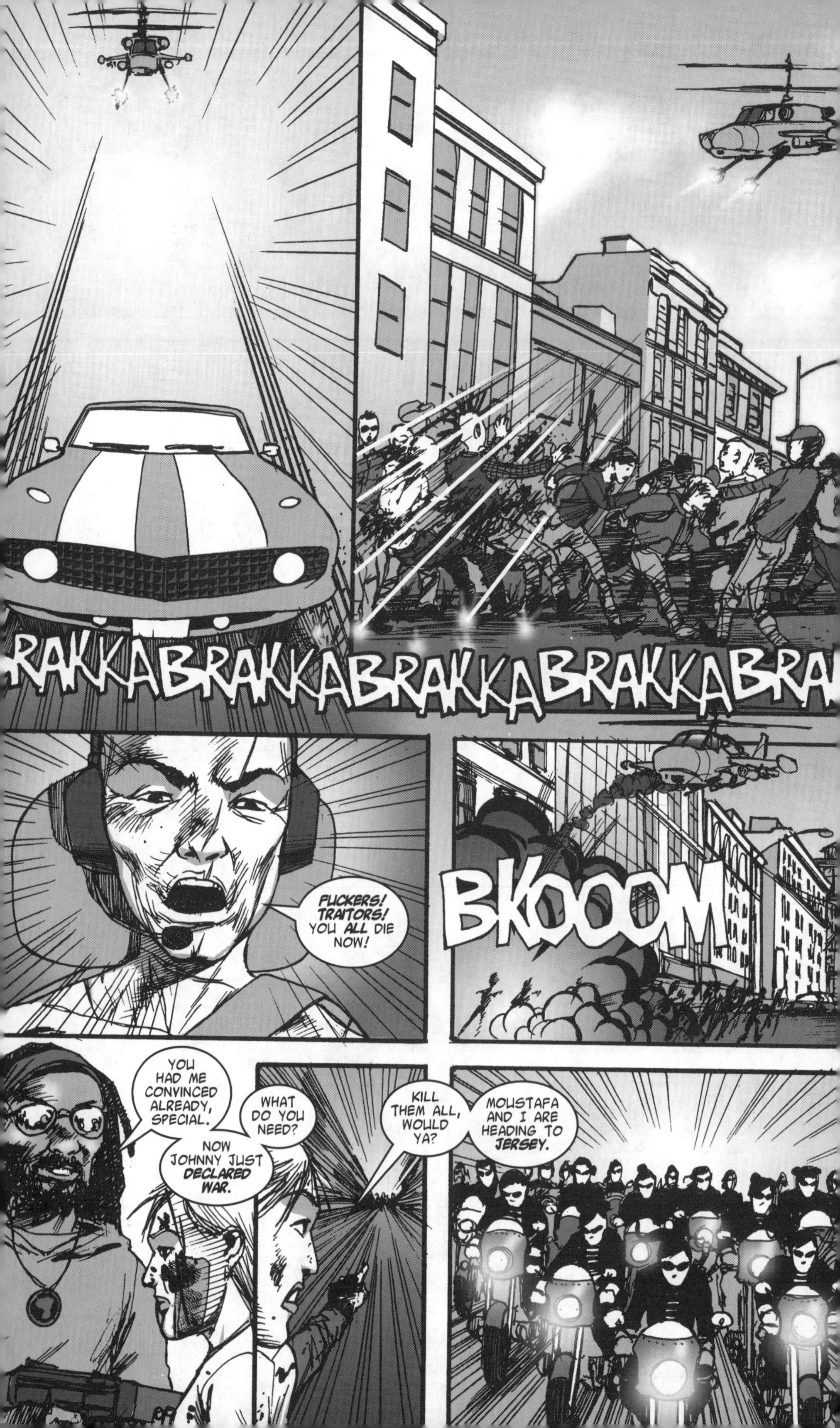
BRAKKABRAKKABRAKKABRAKKABRA
FUCKERS! TRAITORS! YOU ALL DIE NOW!
BKOOOM
YOU HAD ME CONVINCED ALREADY, SPECIAL.
NOW JOHNNY JUST DECLARED WAR.
WHAT DO YOU NEED?
KILL THEM ALL, WOULD YA?
MOUSTAFA AND I ARE HEADING TO JERSEY.

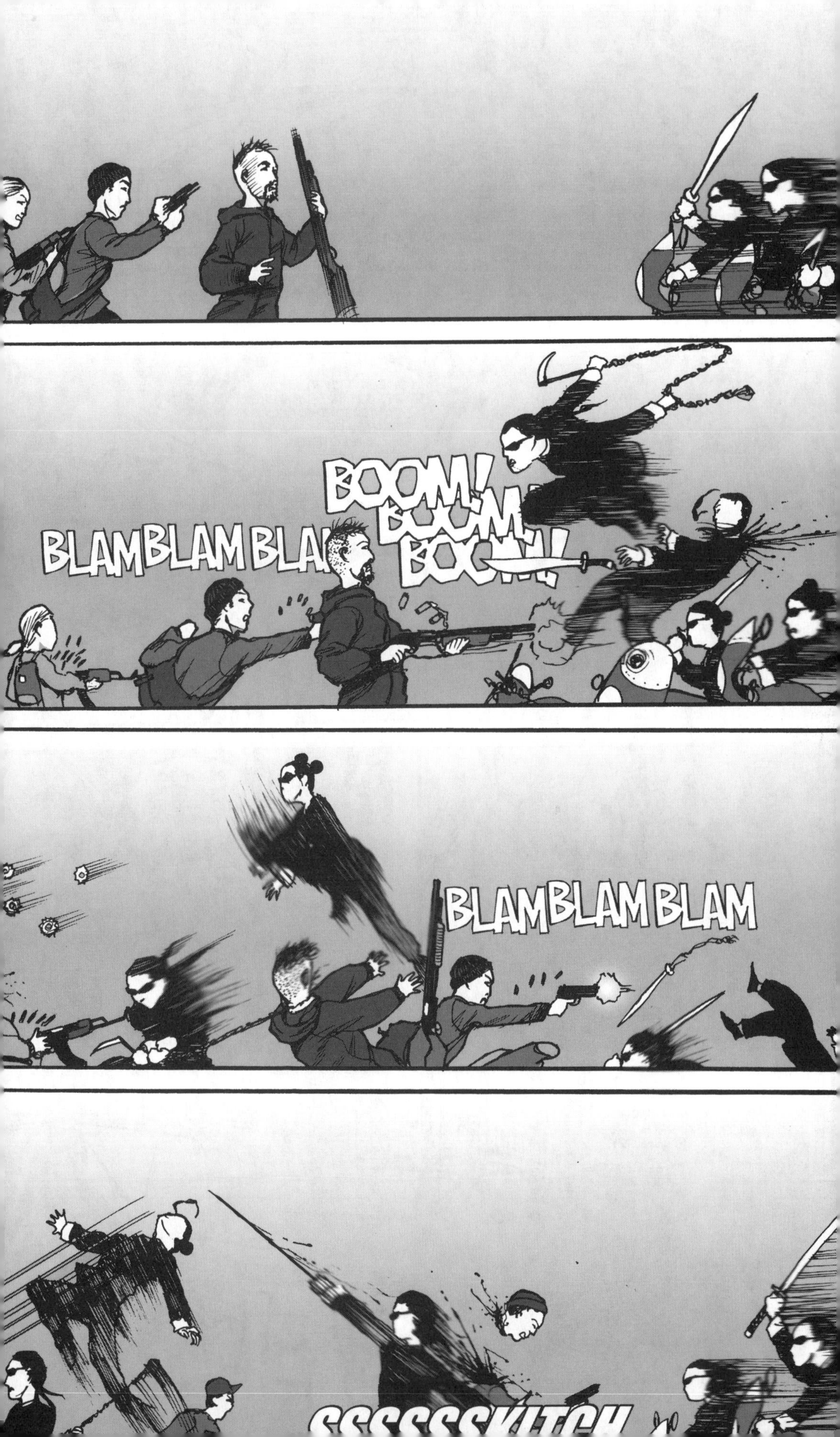
BOOM!
BOOM!
BOO
BLAMBLAMBLA
BLAMBLAMBLAM
SSSSSSKITCH

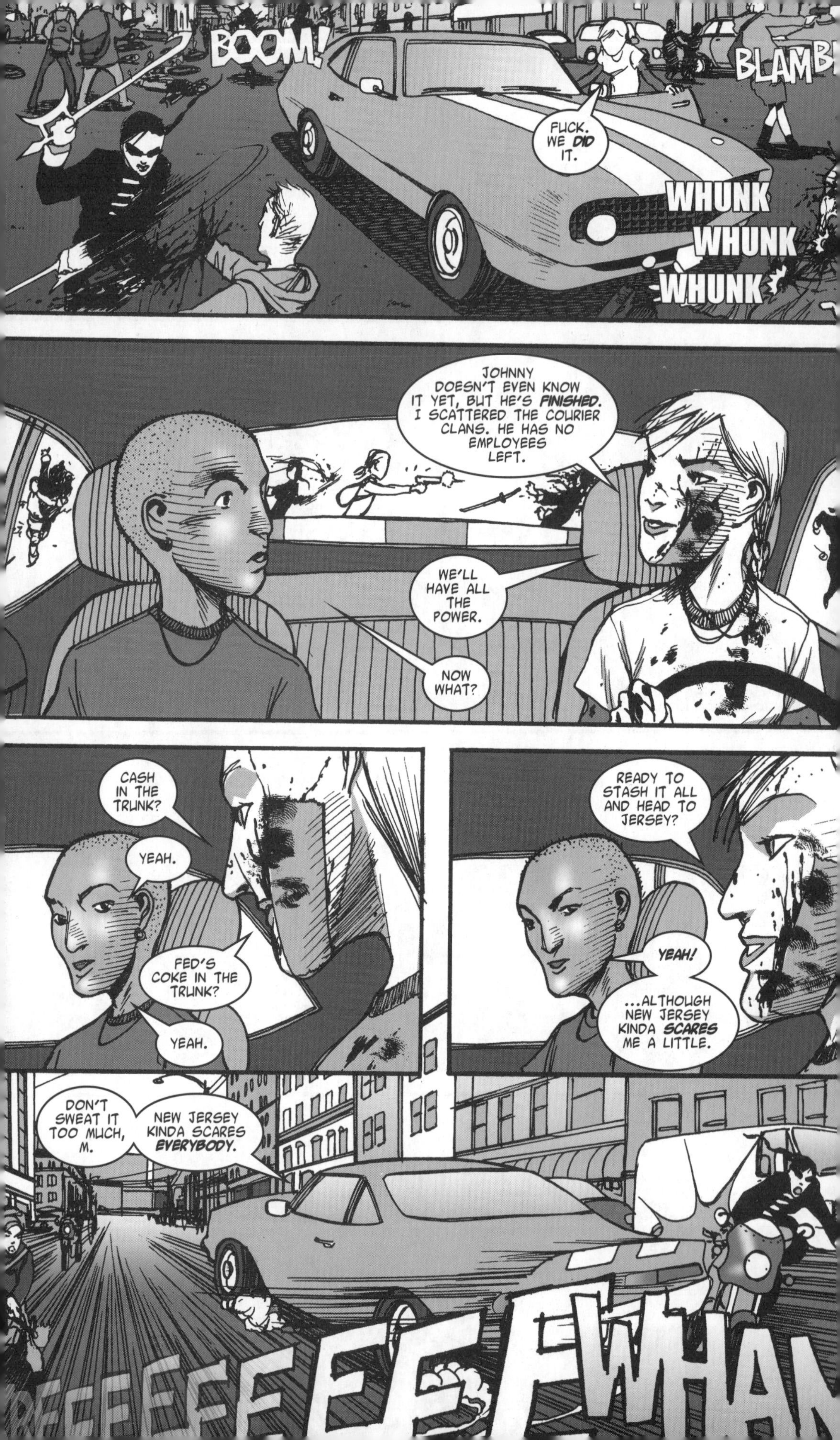
BOOM!
BLAMB
FUCK. WE DID IT.
WHUNK
WHUNK
WHUNK
JOHNNY DOESN'T EVEN KNOW IT YET, BUT HE'S FINISHED. I SCATTERED THE COURIER CLANS. HE HAS NO EMPLOYEES LEFT.
WE'LL HAVE ALL THE POWER.
NOW WHAT?
CASH IN THE TRUNK?
YEAH.
FED'S COKE IN THE TRUNK?
YEAH.
READY TO STASH IT ALL AND HEAD TO JERSEY?
YEAH!
...ALTHOUGH NEW JERSEY KINDA SCARES ME A LITTLE.
DON'T SWEAT IT TOO MUCH, M.
NEW JERSEY KINDA SCARES EVERYBODY.
FWHAN

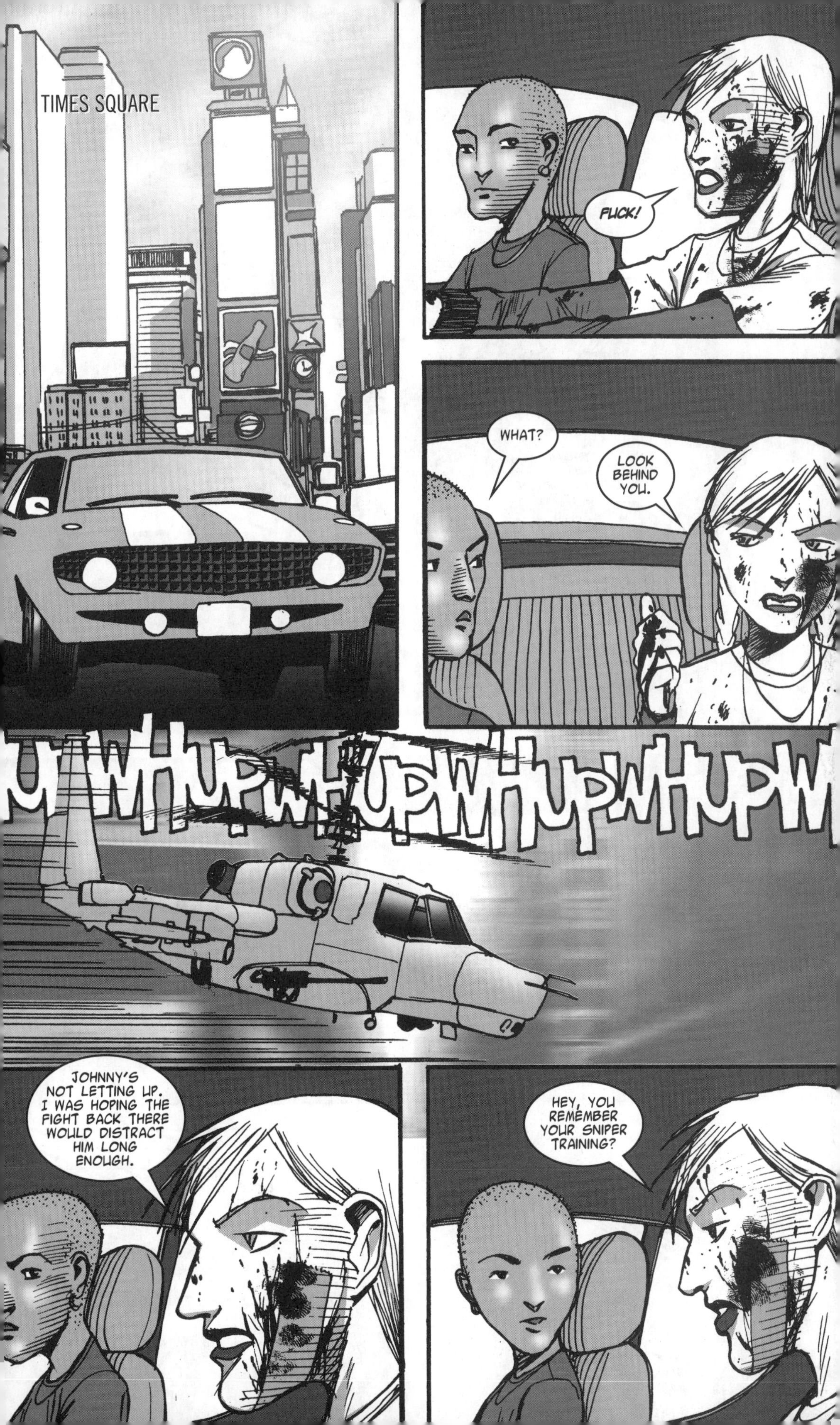
TIMES SQUARE
FUCK!
WHAT?
LOOK BEHIND YOU.
WHUPWHUPWHUPWHUPWHUPW
JOHNNY'S NOT LETTING UP. I WAS HOPING THE FIGHT BACK THERE WOULD DISTRACT HIM LONG ENOUGH.
HEY, YOU REMEMBER YOUR SNIPER TRAINING?

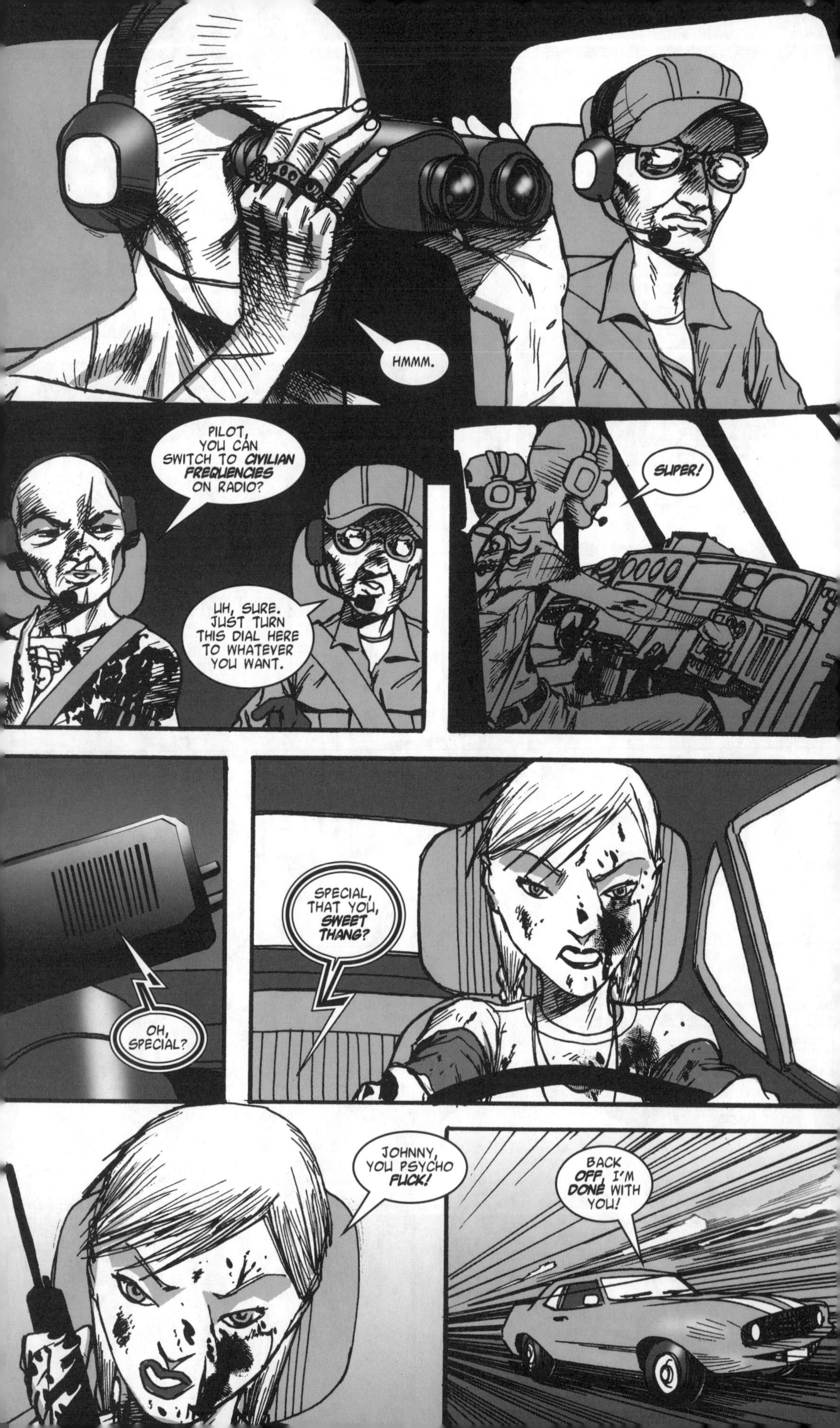
HMMM.
PILOT, YOU CAN SWITCH TO CIVILIAN FREQUENCIES ON RADIO?
UH, SURE. JUST TURN THIS DIAL HERE TO WHATEVER YOU WANT.
SUPER!
OH, SPECIAL?
SPECIAL, THAT YOU, SWEET THANG?
JOHNNY, YOU PSYCHO FUCK!
BACK OFF, I'M DONE WITH YOU!

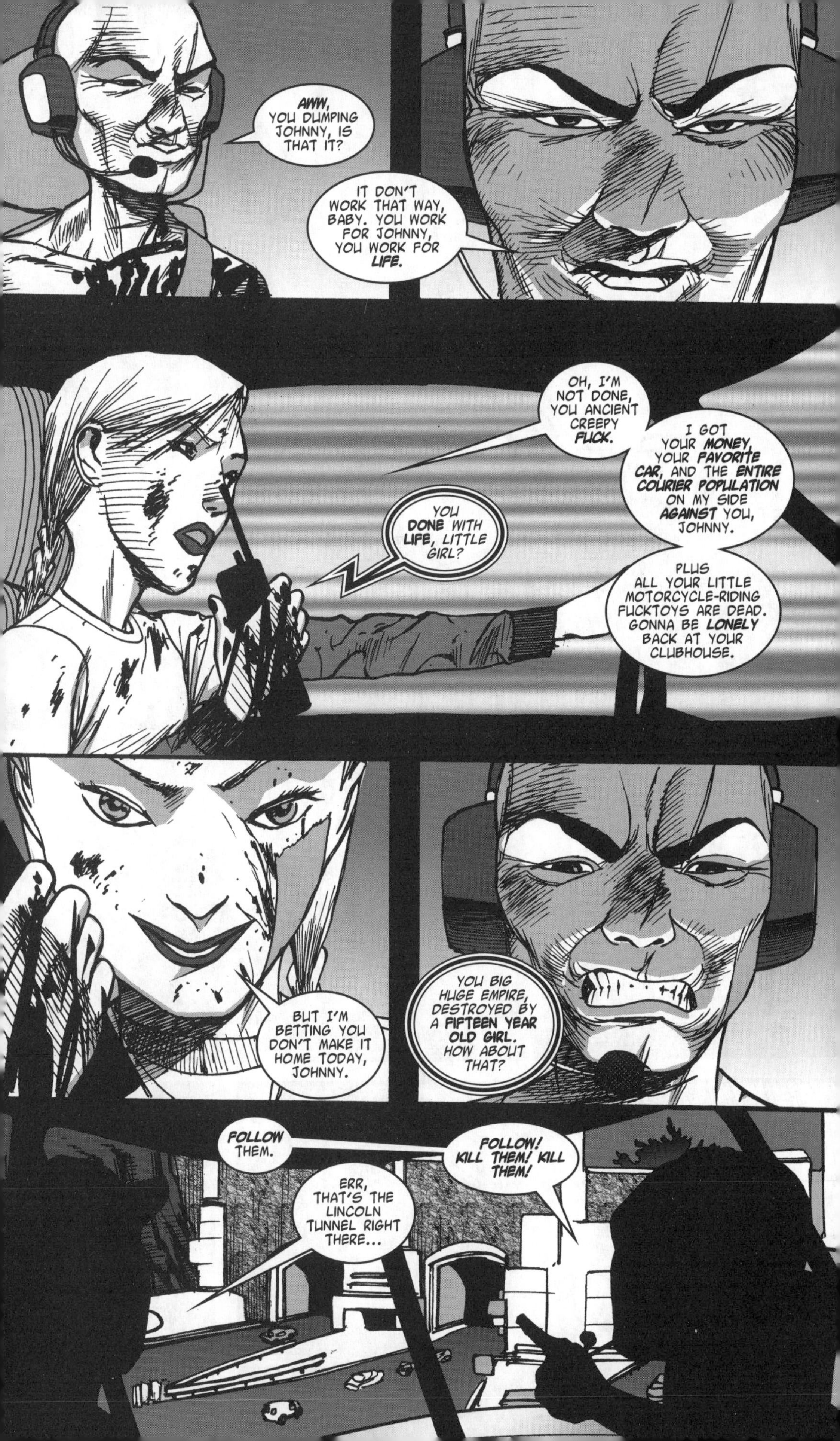
AWW, YOU DUMPING JOHNNY, IS THAT IT?
IT DON'T WORK THAT WAY, BABY. YOU WORK FOR JOHNNY, YOU WORK FOR LIFE.
OH, I'M NOT DONE, YOU ANCIENT CREEPY FUCK.
YOU DONE WITH LIFE, LITTLE GIRL?
I GOT YOUR MONEY, YOUR FAVORITE CAR, AND THE ENTIRE COURIER POPULATION ON MY SIDE AGAINST YOU, JOHNNY.
PLUS ALL YOUR LITTLE MOTORCYCLE-RIDING FUCKTOYS ARE DEAD. GONNA BE LONELY BACK AT YOUR CLUBHOUSE.
BUT I'M BETTING YOU DON'T MAKE IT HOME TODAY, JOHNNY.
YOU BIG HUGE EMPIRE, DESTROYED BY A FIFTEEN YEAR OLD GIRL. HOW ABOUT THAT?
FOLLOW THEM.
FOLLOW! KILL THEM! KILL THEM!
ERR, THAT'S THE LINCOLN TUNNEL RIGHT THERE...

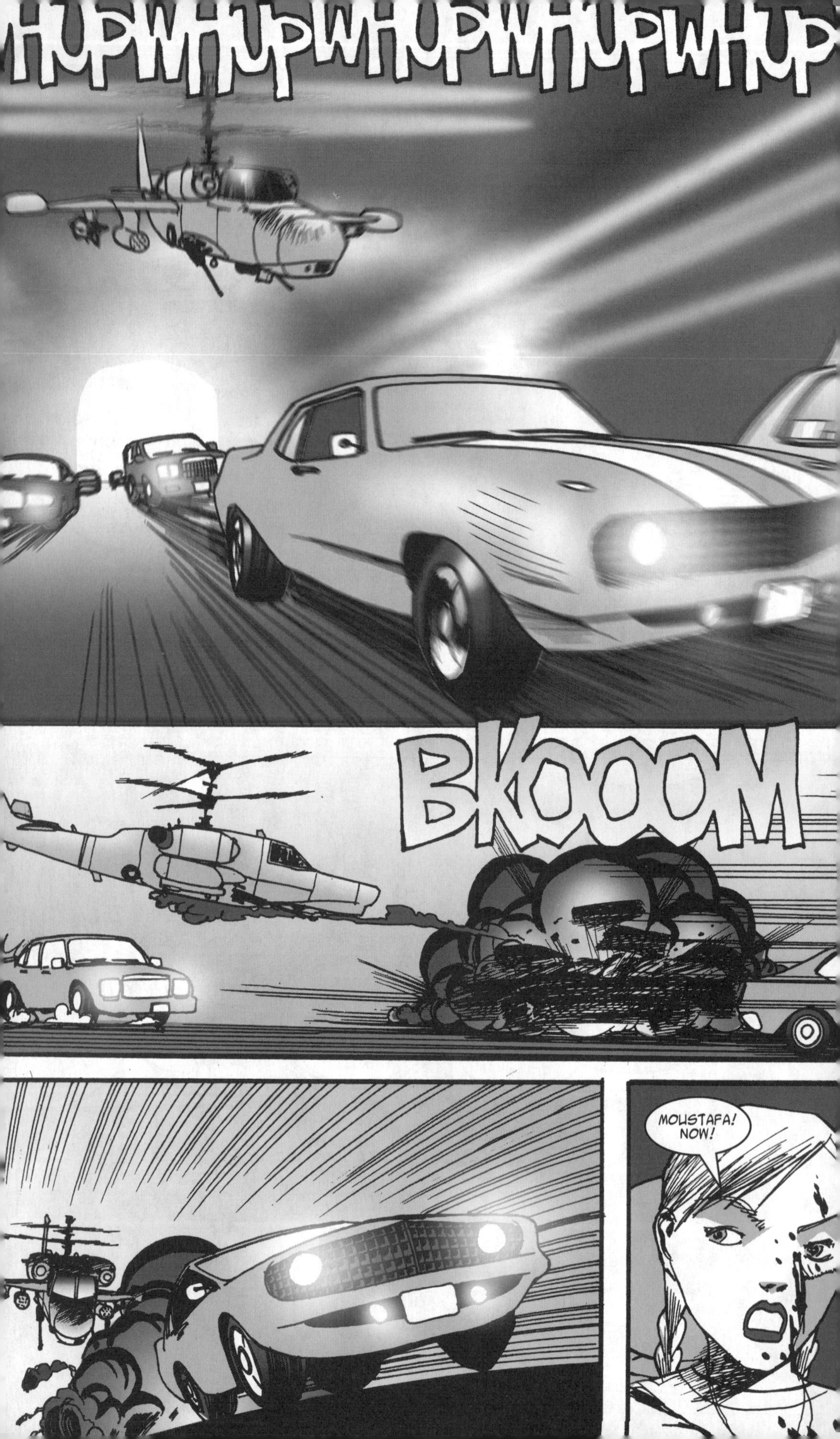
WHUPWHUPWHUPWHUPWHUP
BKOOOM
MOUSTAFA! NOW!

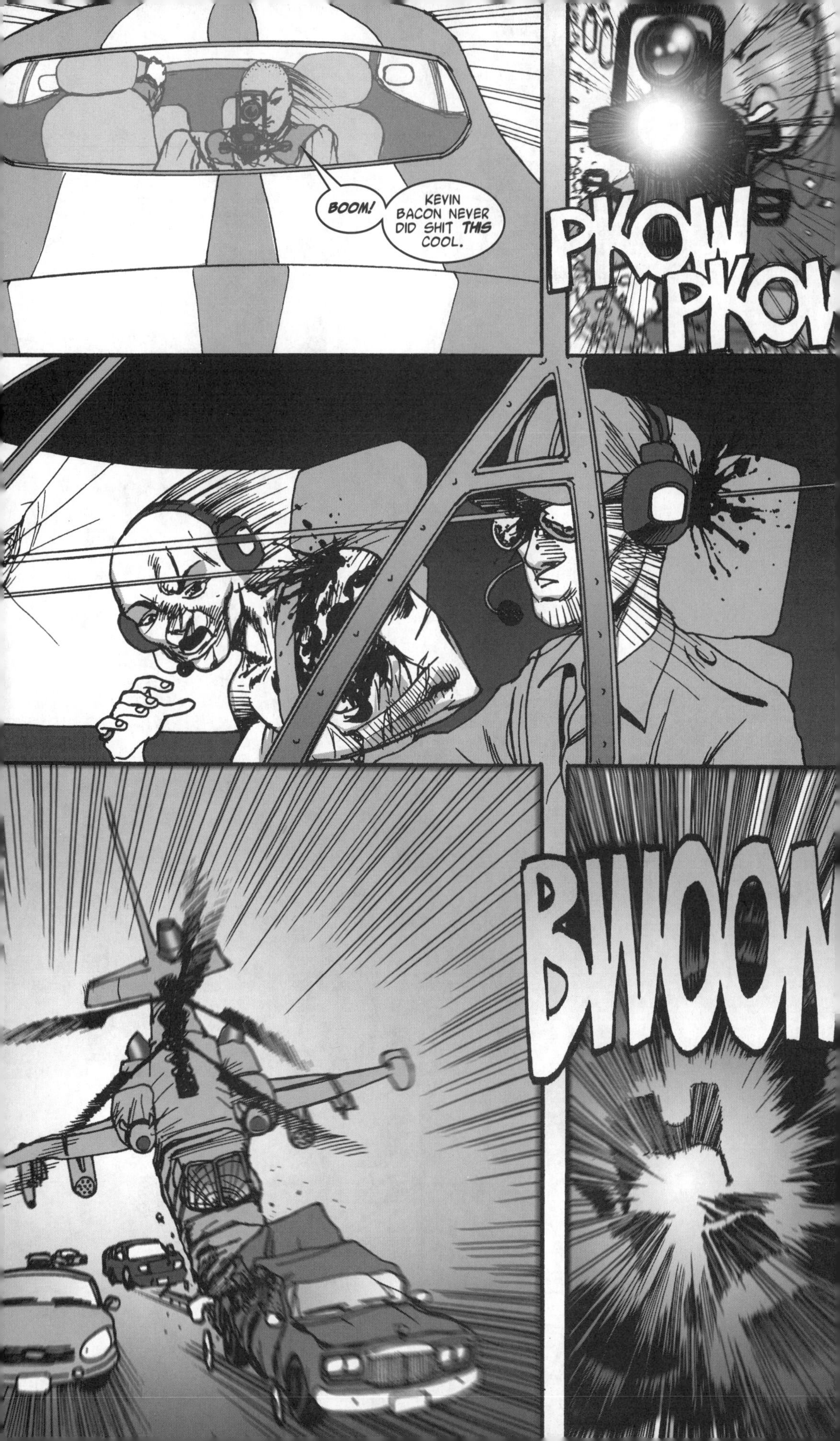
BOOM!
KEVIN BACON NEVER DID SHIT THIS COOL.
PKOW
PKOW
BWOOM

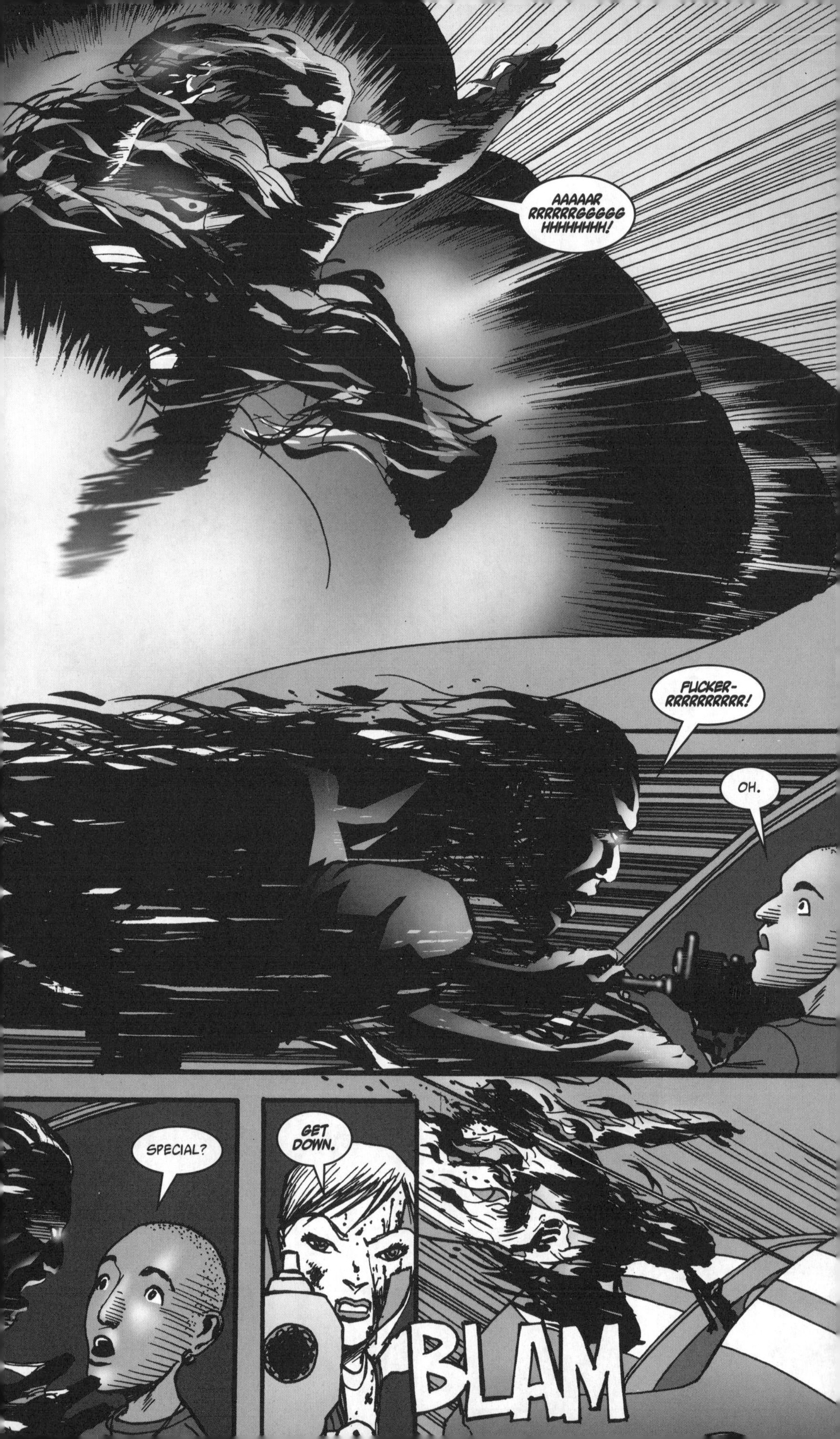
AAAAAR RRRRRRGGGGG HHHHHHHH!
FUCKER-RRRRRRRRRR!
OH.
SPECIAL?
GET DOWN.
BLAM

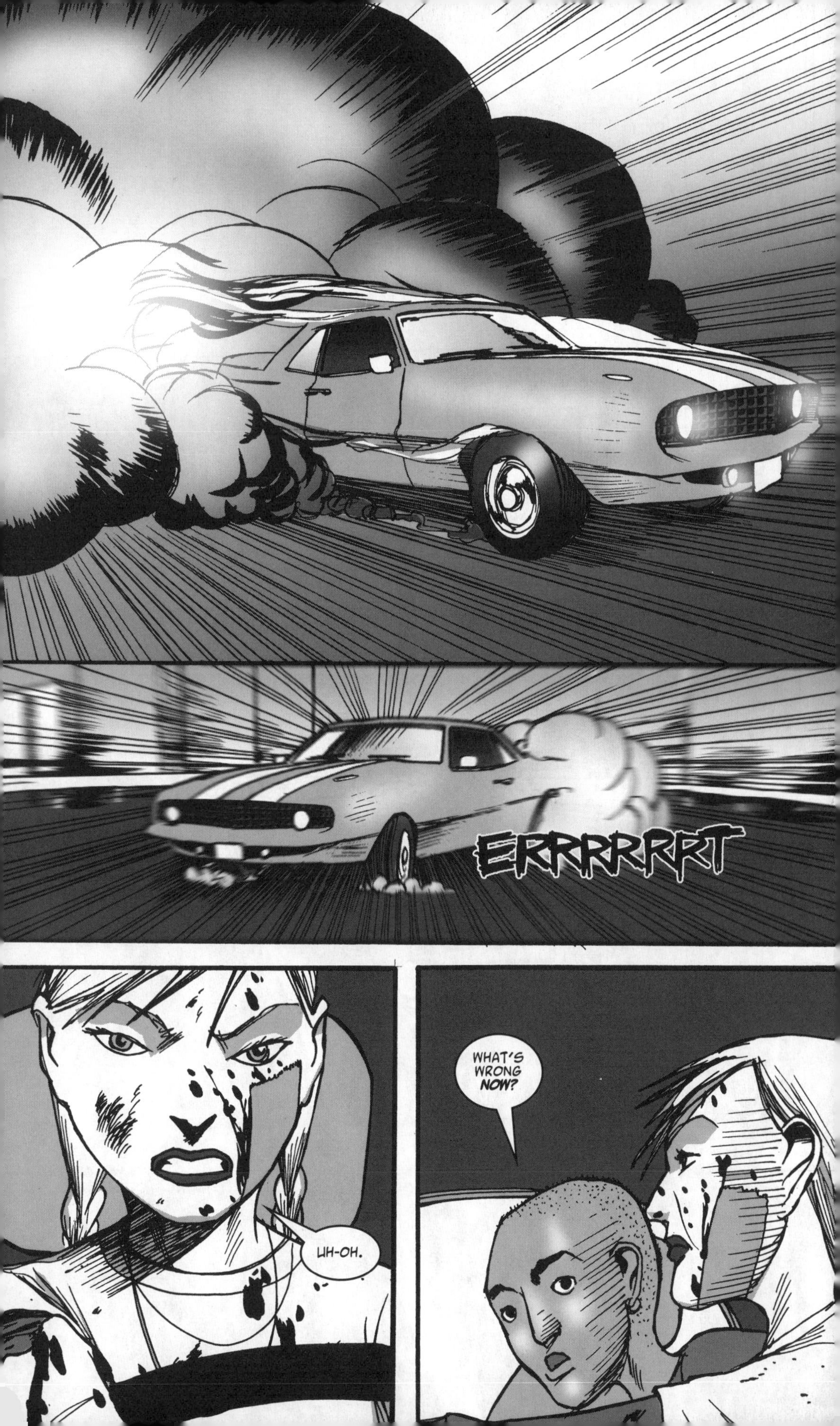
ERRRRRRT
UH-OH.
WHAT'S WRONG NOW?

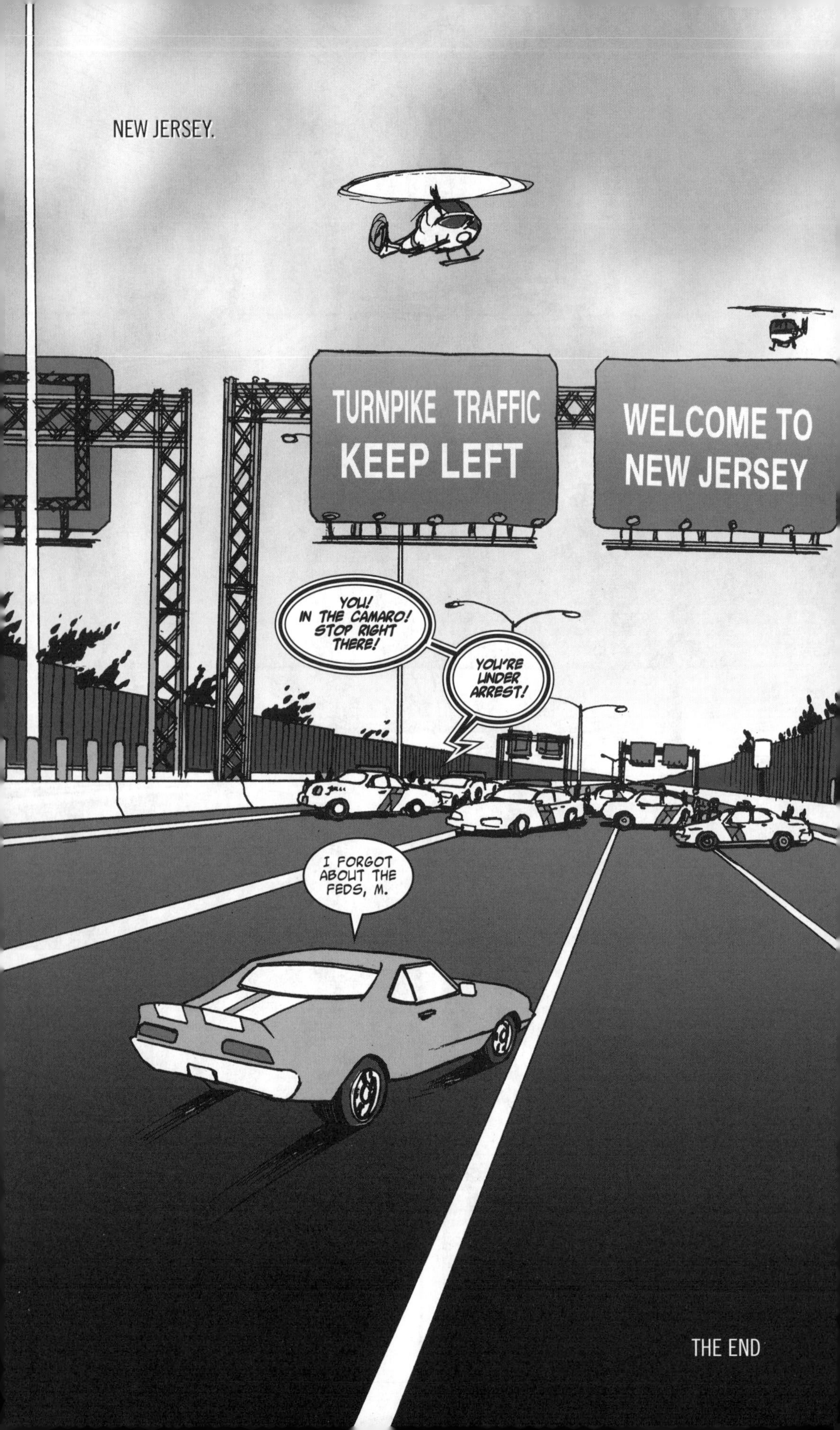
NEW JERSEY.
TURNPIKE TRAFFIC KEEP LEFT
WELCOME TO NEW JERSEY
YOU! IN THE CAMARO! STOP RIGHT THERE!
YOU'RE UNDER ARREST!
I FORGOT ABOUT THE FEDS, M.
THE END

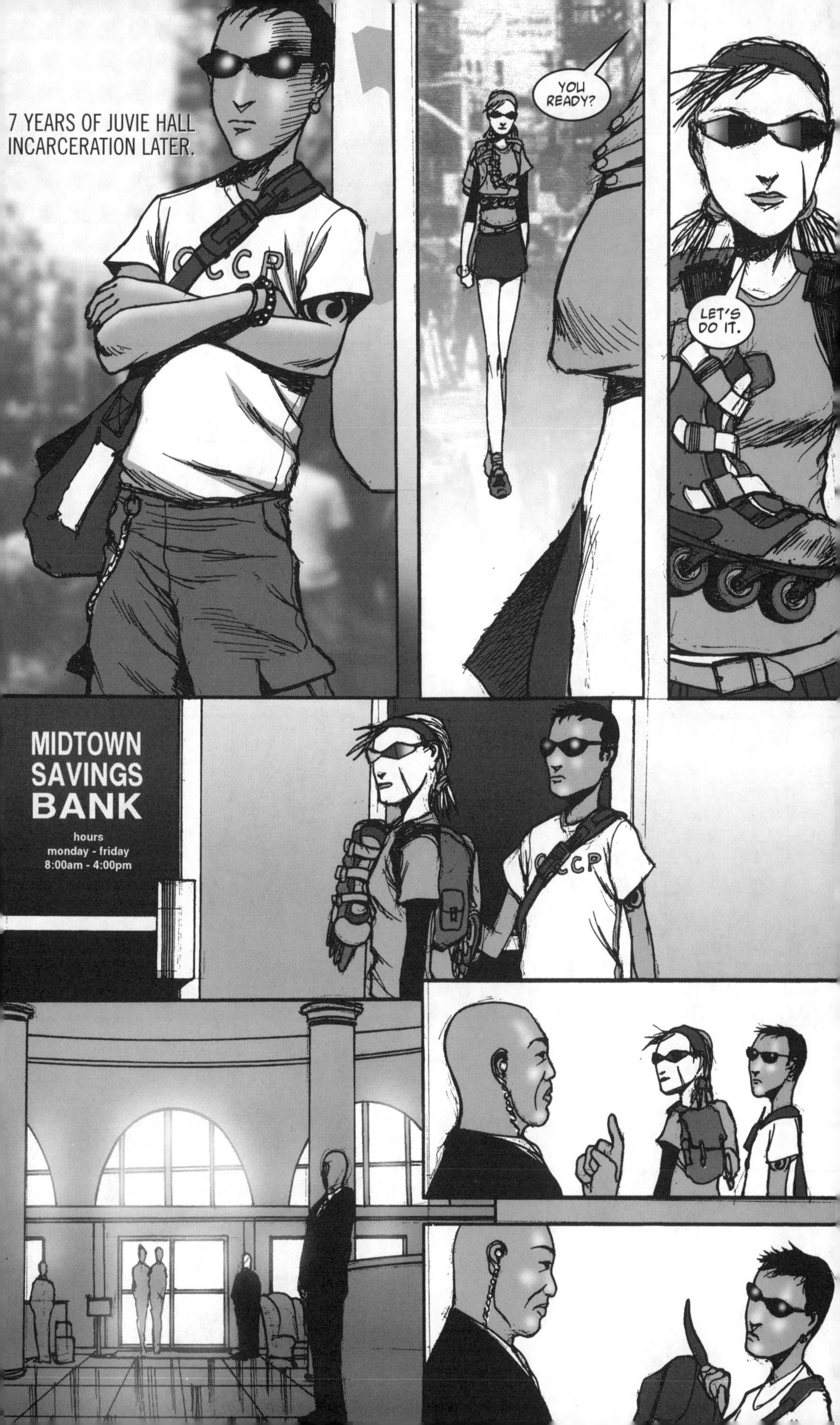
7 YEARS OF JUVIE HALL INCARCERATION LATER.
YOU READY?
LET'S DO IT.
MIDTOWN SAVINGS BANK
hours
monday - friday
8:00am - 4:00pm

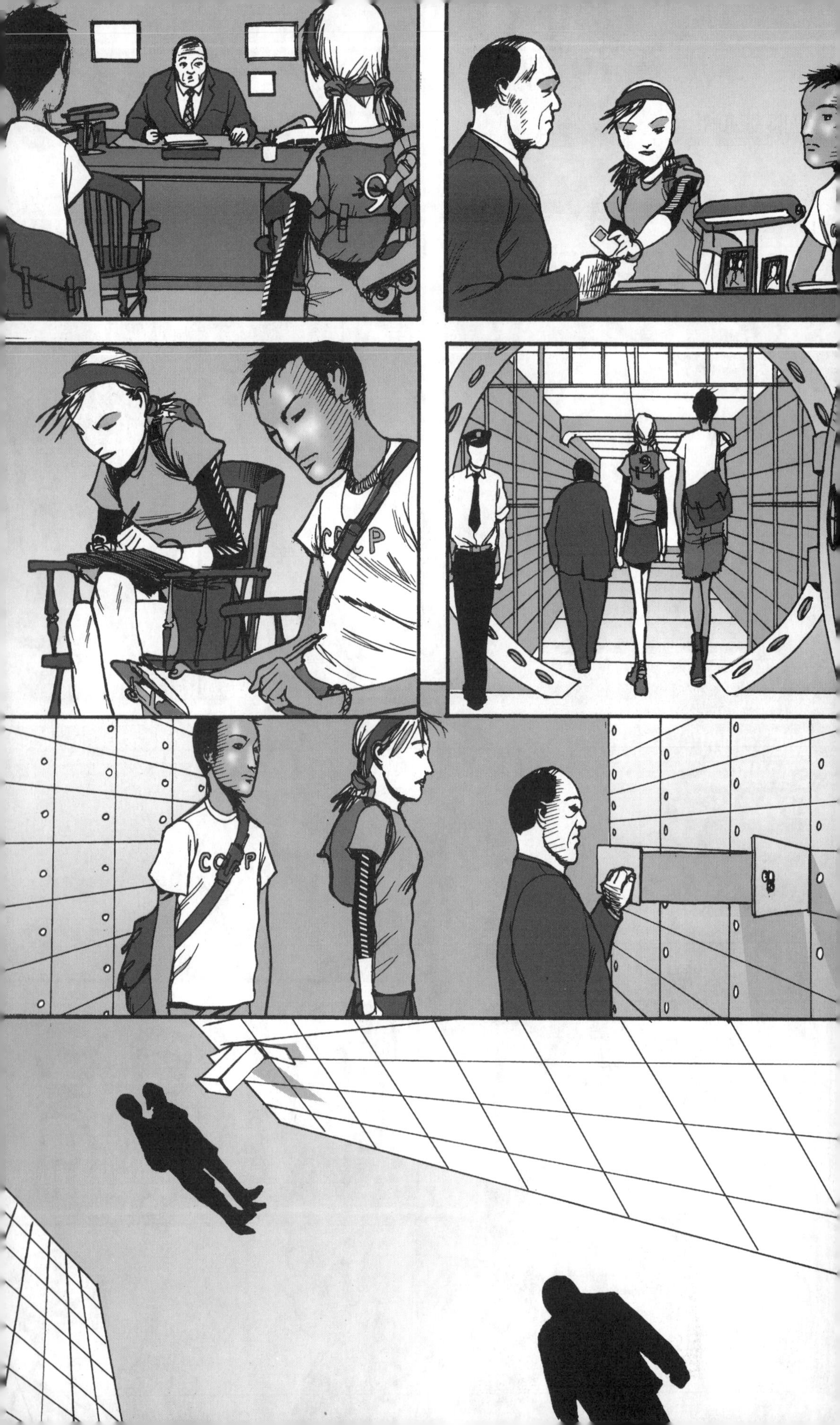

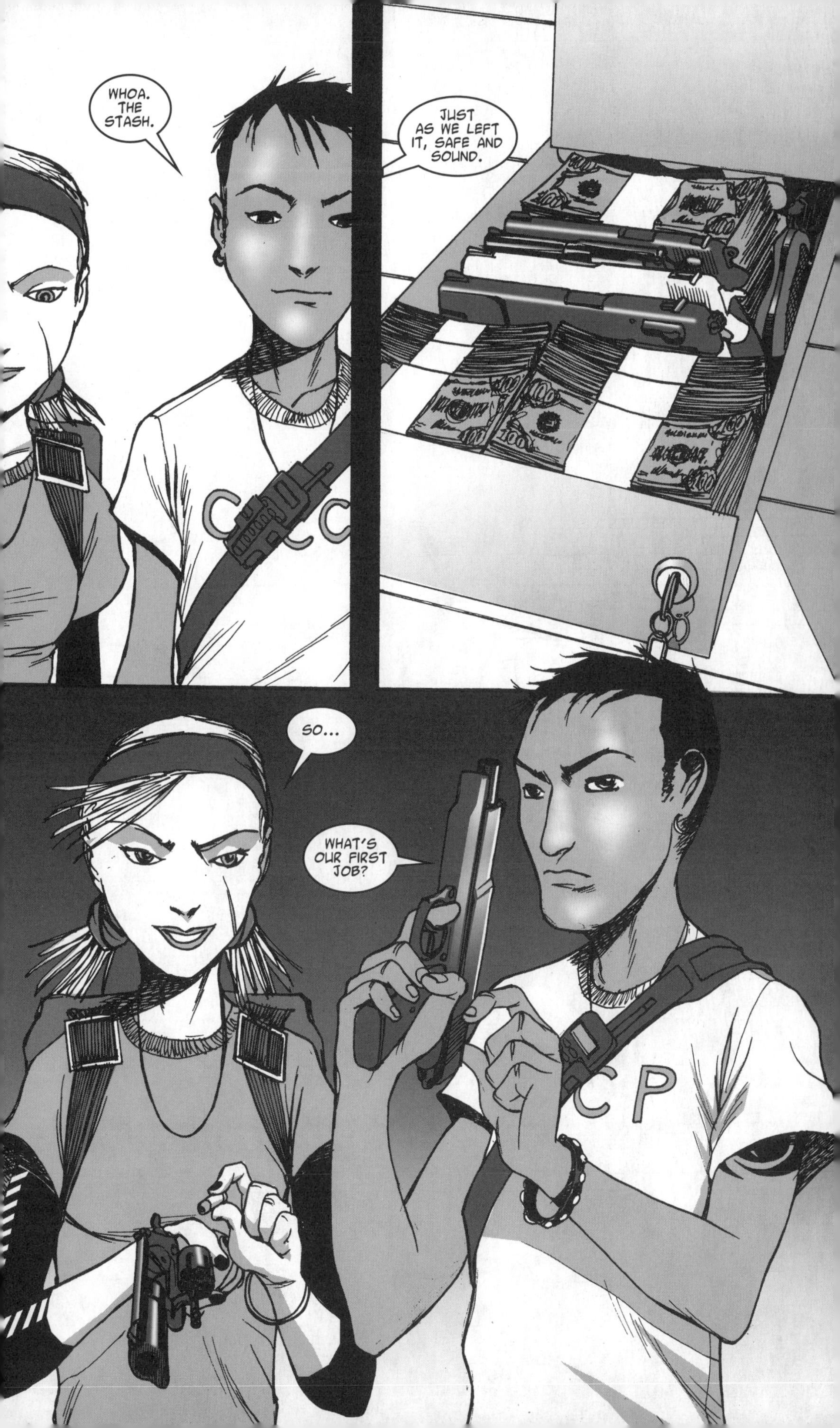
WHOA. THE STASH.
JUST AS WE LEFT IT, SAFE AND SOUND.
SO...
WHAT'S OUR FIRST JOB?

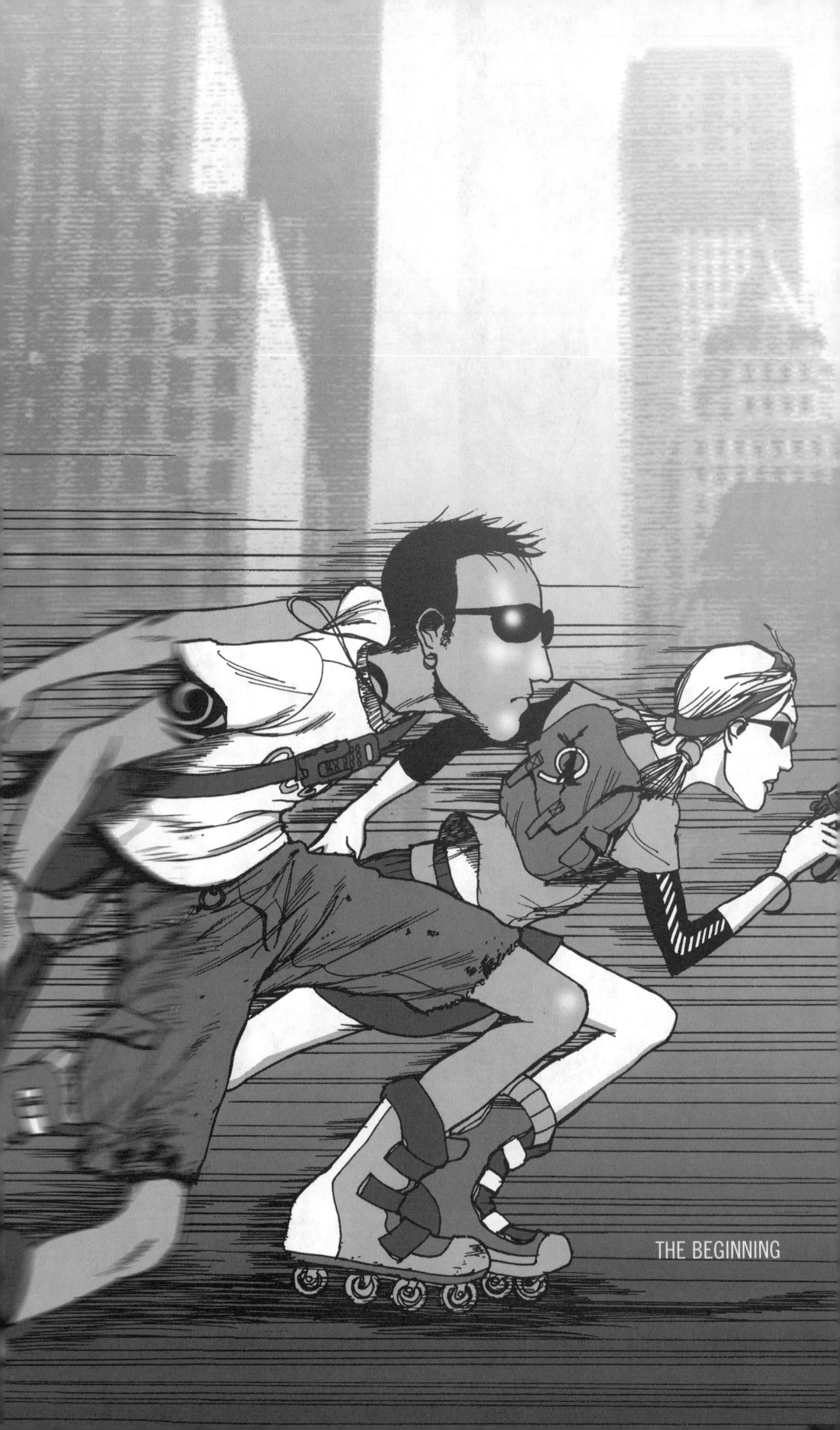
THE BEGINNING

It was a good year...

In 1993, **BRIAN WOOD** was 21, living in the East Village, drinking malt liquor and spending Sunday nights at the Rock-n-Roll Church at Limelight. Since then, Brian's graduated art school, written and drawn a ton of comics, designed for the videogame industry, created a t-shirt company, and is much pickier about the beer he consumes.

In 1993 a 19 year old **ROB G** had an unhealthy obsession with field-hockey players and dreams of becoming a rockstar. These days Rob assaults the comics world with art on titles like DETECTIVE COMICS and TEENAGERS FROM MARS. He lives in Brooklyn with his wife and bunny.

In 1993, **RYAN YOUNT** was 13, and he saved a baby deer from the crushing maw of his pet Irish Wolfhound. This earned him the respect and allegiance of deer everywhere. Currently, Ryan lives in the Sierra Nevada foothills, letters comics, and connects to the internet with two-cans-and-a-string.